Rediscovering Pastoral Care

Rediscovering Pastoral Care

ALASTAIR V. CAMPBELL

Darton, Longman & Todd
London

First published in Great Britain in 1981
Darton, Longman and Todd Ltd
89 Lillie Road
London SW6 1UD

ISBN 0 232 51472 0

British Library Cataloguing in Publication Data

Campbell, Alastair
  Rediscovering pastoral care.
  1. Church work
  I. Title
  253   BV4400

ISBN 0–232–51472–0

Printed in Great Britain by The Anchor Press Ltd
and bound by Wm Brendon & Son Ltd
both of Tiptree, Essex

To Sally

Contents

Acknowledgements

The excerpt from 'Not So. Not So.' by Anne Sexton in *The Awful Rowing Toward God* is reproduced by permission of Houghton Mifflin Co. and the Sterling Lord Agency, © 1975 by Loring Conant, Jr., Executor of the Estate of Anne Sexton.

The excerpt from 'The Second Coming' by W. B. Yeats from *Collected Poems* is reproduced by permission of M. B. Yeats, Anne Yeats and Macmillan London Ltd and Macmillan Inc., New York.

The extracts from 'Burnt Norton', 'East Coker' and 'Little Gidding' by T. S. Eliot from *Four Quartets* are reproduced by permission of Faber and Faber and Harcourt Brace Jovanovich Inc, © 1943 by T. S. Eliot; renewed 1971 by E. V. Eliot.

The excerpts from 'The Fool' by Tessa Stiven in *Poetry of Persons*, published by Quarto Press, are reproduced by permission of the author.

The excerpts from Poem XLVIII from 'Gitanjali' by Rabindranath Tagore are reproduced by permission of Macmillan Co. Ltd, India and the Trustees of the R. Tagore Estate.

The text from the *Good News Bible* is reproduced by permission of the publishers (the Bible Society in association with Collins), O.T. © American Bible Society 1976, N.T. © American Bible Society 1966, 1971, and 1976.

Preface

The origins of this book can be traced back to the unforget-
table two years I spent in San Francisco Theological Semi-
nary in 1962–4 as a Harkness Fellow of the Commonwealth
Fund. Those years opened up an exciting new field of study,
one virtually unknown to the 'classical' theological education
offered in Edinburgh. Even the *names* were new – Pastoral
Counselling, Pastoral Psychology, Clinical Pastoral Education – and the possibility of combining psychological and
theological concepts had all the attractiveness of hitherto forbidden fruit. For the insights I gained into these disciplines
I am deeply grateful to my friends and teachers, Aaron Un-
gersma, Roy Fairchild and (especially) Ted Stein.

But that original stimulus has taken a long time to have its
full effect. Despite an obligation to teach the subject to divin-
ity students for over a decade, it took a new stimulus to make
me put my own thoughts into writing. (In the interim the
fascinating ethical issues in medicine and health care had
captured my attention.) This second stimulus came from an
invitation to lead the annual Pastoral Care Workshop spon-
sored by the Chaplaincy Department of the Royal Perth Hospital, Western Australia. This was followed by an invitation
to lead the Biennial Conference of the New Zealand Hospital
Chaplains' Association in Auckland. These invitiations came
just at the right time for me, since I had been toying with
rough outlines for a book on pastoral care for too long. The
need to prepare a set of reasonably coherent public lectures
doth wonderfully concentrate the mind! I would like to express my thanks to many colleagues and friends in Australia
and New Zealand for their warm encouragement and numerous creative suggestions during my visit there, most especially

to Roger Ryall, Roy Bradley, Douglas Kidd and Jim Battersby.

The field of pastoral care overlaps virtually all the other theological disciplines at one point or another. I have therefore turned to several colleagues for help and advice, but since I have also taken several risks in interpretation (solely on my own judgement), they must certainly be absolved from any responsibility for the errors of my inadequate scholarship. Among those who advised me were Hugh Anderson, Graeme Auld, John Cumming, Alan Lewis, David Lyall, Elizabeth Templeton and Ian Thompson. My colleague Duncan Forrester has been particularly supportive throughout, not only by commenting on the early drafts, but by providing the kind of simple encouragement which is the heart of good companionship. Finally Elma Webster has been of invaluable help, by giving up many hours to the labour of typing successive drafts, and by responding with interest and enthusiasm to the material she was typing.

This book begins with the question: How may we rediscover pastoral care in our age? I do not hope to have provided a definitive answer. But if I have succeeded in shifting the debate back into the *theological* arena, I shall be more than happy.

Edinburgh
November 1980   Alastair V. Campbell

1

Pastoral Care: A Question Of Integrity

He fed them according to the integrity of his heart;
and guided them by the skilfulness of his hands.

Psalm 78: 72 AV

This book is concerned with the rediscovery of pastoral care, a rediscovery made necessary by a contemporary sense of confusion about the true nature of Christian caring and by a feeling of alienation from traditional understandings of the pastoral task. The confusion has been partly caused by the extraordinary successes of the 'sciences of man' – in particular psychology and sociology – in shedding light on the causes of human distress and the nature of helping relationships. This makes us feel that we now have a much more sophisticated view of social interaction and of the ambiguities of care and counselling than the simple rural image of a shepherd tending his flock, from which the phrase 'pastoral care' derives. At the same time there are aspects of the pastoral care tradition, in particular its stress on priestly or ministerial authority and on the helplessness of the Christian 'flock', which alienate us. As men and women 'come of age' we find ourselves reacting against what we regard as the unwarranted paternalism and judgementalism of our forefathers. We want to discover a style of Christian caring which treats us as adults, not as errant children or feckless sheep, and which acknowledges the ambiguity of every offer of care in a situation of *mutual* responsibility and *mutual* need.

Yet the temptation to discard everything from the past as irrelevant to our present situation must be resisted. This would be an adolescent reaction to the views of past generations, as immature and inadequate as the false antiquarianism which treats the tradition as sacrosanct. Much recent pastoral care literature seems to have been so enamoured of 'psycho-dynamic' insights and 'counselling methodologies' that it refers to the Christian theological heritage only in passing and then only in a functional way, in the search for what are called 'religious resources'.[1] The tradition deserves more careful attention than that! In the first section of this chapter I shall explore (very briefly and inadequately) some aspects of the recent past which seem to cause this sense of alienation, in the hope of discovering the lineaments of a modern understanding which has truly come to terms with its past.

ALIENATION FROM THE TRADITION

In a recent book, Harvey Cox has suggested that the lessons to be learned from the history of Christian orthodoxy are largely negative:

> . . . we should read it more as a cautionary tale than as a treasure house of available inspiration. We Christians today need to understand our history as a compulsive neurotic needs to understand his – in order to see where we veered off, lost genuine options, glimpsed something we were afraid to pursue, or denied who we really are.[2]

Cox goes on to suggest that we can learn more from heretics and schismatics than from the orthodox: 'Their vision may have been too early for their time, but it is not too early for ours.'

A quite different view of the situation has been taken by Thomas C. Oden in a paper commenting specifically on the absence in modern pastoral counselling literature of any interest in the classical models of pastoral care:

> Recent pastoral counselling has incurred a fixated dependency and indebtedness to modern psychology and to modern consciousness generally that has prevented it from even looking at pre-modern wisdoms of most kinds including classical pastoral care. . . . We have bet all our chips on the assumption that modern consciousness will lead us into vaster freedom, while our specific freedom to be attentive to the Christian pastoral tradition has been plundered, polemicised and despoiled.[3]

Both Cox and Oden seem to me to be presenting unnecessarily extreme views of the situation. It is important to identify much more specifically the reasons for our discomfort with the tradition before passing judgement on our attitudes to it.

In their excellent historical survey and selection of readings from the classical documents, W. A. Clebsch and C. R. Jaekle have tried to 'assist in the recovery of a sense of the richness and variety of Christian pastoral care as it has been exercised in the past', but they have also pointed to the obstacles to such a recovery. I shall expand upon three of the obstacles arising from contemporary Christian self-understanding to which Clebsch and Jaekle briefly refer: absence of theological consensus; awareness of the complexity of human motivation; and uncertainty about the pastoral role.[4]

Absence of Theological Consensus

Within the Reformed tradition of pastoral care there has always been an emphasis on the teaching role of the pastor, whether in the pulpit or in the homes of 'his people'. (We recall Edwin Muir's wry summary of Scottish Calvinism: 'The Word made flesh here is made word again.')[5] A good example of this tradition is to be found in Richard Baxter's *Gildas Silvianus* or *The Reformed Pastor*. Baxter lists seven pastoral functions: conversion of the unconverted; advice to enquirers; building up the already converted; oversight of families in the congregation; visiting the sick; reproof of the impenitent; exercise of discipline.[6] A powerful stress on right doctrine, and on the minister as overseer and teacher is evident from this list. Moreover, formal catechizing had an important place in the pastor's regular oversight of all the families in the congregation. Baxter's whole approach to pastoral care is summed up in a phrase of a twentieth-century Barthian theologian, Eduard Thurneysen, 'Communication to the individual of the message proclaimed in general to the congregation in the sermon'.[7]

Yet already by the nineteenth century the directive emphasis in this approach was clearly yielding to the 'acids of modernity'. Thus Patrick Fairbairn, first Principal of the Free Church College in Glasgow, rejects the practice of catechizing, partly because people will no longer accept it and partly because it is 'held merely as the buttress and ornament of a lifeless orthodoxy'. As regards the practice of investigating the spiritual welfare of families before Communion he has this to say:

> . . . there has come, along with other changes in the course of time, such a divided state of things in parishes and families, such an impatience of authority and whatever in matters of religion wears an inquisitorial aspect . . . as renders the spirit only, not the precise form, of the good old practice for the most part applicable in our generation.[8]

This quotation foreshadows the modern era, in which the whole notion of a monolithic orthodoxy is under question. Our age is far from unique in having divergent theological opinions, as even a cursory study of church history will show, but there is now an increasing tendency to *welcome* pluralism and imprecision in doctrine rather than to deplore it. Appreciation of the complexity of truth, tolerance of ambiguity, and awareness that all theoretical formulations only approximate to the reality they attempt to describe are regarded as marks of the educated intellect.[9] Faith is experienced as a *quest* for understanding, requiring a constant renewal of theological categories to do it justice.

Of course, the notion of *instruction* in 'the faith' still remains as an element in modern pastoral care. As the quotation from Thurneysen has already indicated, Barth's theology of the Word of God heralded a revival of the concept of authoritative proclamation and a rejection of the 'liberal' reliance on human capacities for spiritual enlightenment.[10] The more conservative Protestant churches have also retained an emphasis on the authority of the minister's teaching role, though frequently this is now set in the context of modified versions of contemporary counselling theory.[11] Nevertheless, however much some theologians and churchmen might wish it otherwise, the absence of doctrinal unanimity – and the *welcoming* of this – remains a feature of our time.

Here then is the first barrier between us and the tradition. We are becoming increasingly aware that our contemporaries are engaged in an individualistic search for truth which reacts against all claims to an inerrant teaching authority. Yet the tradition sees teaching as an integral aspect of pastoral care. We shall surmount this barrier only by a reassessment of the nature of teaching and learning. A teacher's authority lies in his ability to transcend the limitations of the individual subject's present awareness. He confronts the learner with something new, yet he does it in a way that allows the learner to make it a genuine part of his own understanding. Teaching thus defined is in essence a transaction between persons. A teacher's authority as a teacher does not depend merely upon the information he possesses, but also upon his ability to make others respond to that information. Teaching in the form of *indoctrination* endeavours to evoke a response of unquestioning acceptance in the learner, presenting this as the attitude of the teacher himself to what he is saying. On the other hand teaching in the form of *exploration* endeavours to evoke a questioning and searching response in the learner. This is done by communicating something of the teacher's own struggle to understand, his own need to be a learner as well as a teacher.

Thus the rediscovery of this aspect of pastoral care at the present time depends upon a different understanding of the character of a teacher's authority. We have gone through a period of nervousness about *any* kind of directiveness, *any* notion that the individual needs to learn through an encounter with that which is other than himself. We cannot return to simplistic contrasts between the knowledgeable and the ignorant, the wise and the foolish. But equally we must question the naive idea that we learn nothing from others, other than that which we already implicitly know ourselves. Instead of either of these extremes, I shall be suggesting that teachers must be *companions* on the same journey that we ourselves are making, and that their authority derives from their ability to be fellow travellers, friends and comrades on this journey. (see Chapter Seven).

The Complexity of Motivation
Difficulties with the tradition increase when we consider the problem of moral judgement in pastoral care. The literature from the past appears to us to make judgements about human actions all too readily and swiftly, ignoring the ambiguities and complexities of motivation. An obvious example may be found in the letters of spiritual counsel written by the Anglican divine, John Keble, to a lady distressed by 'the absence of conscious love and devotion' for God. Keble at first tries to persuade her to ignore this 'morbid feeling'. When this

fails, he grows somewhat impatient with her persistent unhappiness:

> ... I must put it to your own conscience, whether there is not in it somewhat of self-tormenting and wilful peevishness. ... I must beg you to ask yourself whether you are really endeavouring to shake off the morbid feelings which haunt you, as sincerely as you would endeavour to cure a toothache.[12]

The hundred years or so which have elapsed since this letter was written seem a very great distance indeed. We would now no doubt suspect that the lady is suffering from some form of neurotic depression, which cannot be so easily 'shaken off'. Rather than appealing to her 'conscience', we would be inclined to search for underlying causes for her low mood.

The sense of distance from the past increases when we consider traditional approaches to the problem of sin and repentance. This element in pastoral care was of central importance from the earliest times, when the Church had to deal with the issue of post-baptismal sin and particularly with the contentious question of the readmission to membership of those who had defected under the Roman persecutions. In subsequent church history, penance, both in public and in private forms, retained great importance and was closely related to receiving the sacrament of Holy Communion. Two examples from the post-Reformation era will serve to illustrate how this tradition has become problematic in modern times.

The first example is the revival of the ancient practice of *public* penance which John Knox introduced to the Church of Scotland, laying down an appropriate form of worship in *The Book of Common Order* of 1564. In the Preface to the Form of Public Repentance, Knox distinguished between 'more heinous' offences – fornication, habitual drunkenness, swearing, fighting, brawling, contempt of the order of the Church, breaking the Sabbath – which always required an act of public penance before the whole congregation; and the 'less heinous but deserving of admonition' – vain words, uncomely gestures, negligence in attending church, suspicion of avarice or pride, superfluity or riotousness in expression of the face or raiment – which required only a private reproof, unless the offender refused to repent and amend his ways, in which case he would eventually be summoned to a public appearance.

In both cases the ultimate punishment for those refusing to submit to the discipline of the Church was excommunication.[13]

The use of public penance as a means of discipline was common in the seventeenth and early eighteenth centuries. Several appearances were by then required depending on the seriousness of the offence.[14] By the nineteenth century, however, the practice had become virtually extinct, although it was not formally abolished until an act of Assembly of 1902. Writing in 1875 Patrick Fairbairn observes that public penance was out of place in the 'civilisation and refinement of modern times . . . things would appear unseemly and indelicate in present times . . . and tend rather to annoy than to edify, which at an earlier period would have been heard or witnessed without emotion'.[15]

For us in the twentieth century, however, the problem is not the offence to propriety of public penance but its encouragement to judgementalism. Certainly in his *Form of Public Repentance* Knox had no thought of identifying the penitent as a greater sinner than the other members of the congregation. The congregation were told, '. . . we (shall) in the sin of this our brother accuse and damn our own sins, in his fall . . . consider and lament our sinful nature . . . knowing that no flesh can be justified before God's presence if the judgement proceed without mercy'.[16] But the identification of *specific offences* and the procedures of accusation, trial before the Session and public denunciation inevitably encourage a legalistic and simplistic view of sin. Such practices obscure the subtleties of human behaviour and allow people the easy comfort of apportioning blame to certain types of action for the sense of human failure in which we should all participate.

A similar problem arises if we consider the practice of private penance, which has persisted (with periods of revival and decline) in the Roman and the Anglican communions for many centuries. An example may be taken from the revival of interest in sacramental penance in the Oxford Movement in the Church of England in the nineteenth century. Edward Pusey, one of the Movement's founders, published a translation of a French manual of confession by Abbé Jean Joseph Gaume. The manual sought to make clear the obligations of the father confessor to the penitent. The picture which emerges is that of a kindly, but authoritative father figure, who must not hesitate to point out to people the error of their ways:

> Above all things, use the greatest charity towards sinners, both in receiving them, and inspiring them with confidence in God's mercy. But never let any human respect hinder you from warning them earnestly, or pointing out their evil condition, and the most suitable means for breaking the chains of their evil habits. Be firm in refusing absolution when it is necessary to do so.[17]

Such certainty in identifying the faults of others now seems a dangerous attitude for anyone to adopt. How can we be so sure that we can judge our fellows? Indeed, can we be sure that, in this modern age, notions like sin, the fall of man, the necessity for repentance and forgiveness carry any meaning at all?

To overcome these difficulties with traditional approaches to sin we need to discover a contemporary understanding of penance and penitence. Perhaps we rightly shy away from an *imposed* penitence, from a heavy-handed judgement on others which reduces them to the status of errant children requiring interrogation and hard discipline, but this should not prevent us from pointing the way and leading the way to a positive form of penitence, which goes *through* the complexity of human motivation not away from it. We get a clue to this positive way of penitence in Nicolas Berdyaev's discussion of a form of asceticism, which could re-establish spiritual awareness in contemporary life:

> The only justifiable asceticism is that which liberates man and restores him to authentic realities. Asceticism should restore man's dignity, not plunge him into a hopeless state of indignity and baseness. . . . The ontological justification of asceticism is its achievement of simplicity or wholeness, of freedom from complexity or disintegration. But the achievement of Divine simplicity implies not the annihilation of the complex world, but its illumination and trans-figuration, its integration in a higher unity. This will involve the appearance of a new type of saint, who will take upon himself the burden of the complex world.[18]

'The burden of the complex world' is perhaps our way of penance, just as our sin is our tendency to avoid that burden

8

with the empty consolations of materialism or of other-worldly pietism. Sin is really no stranger to us, but we need to learn its name afresh and to recognize its manifestations in our age. Thus the rediscovery of pastoral care must include a fresh understanding of both guilt and grace.

Uncertainty about the Pastoral Role

If we find difficulties with the traditional emphases on cate-chesis and penance in pastoral care, it is hardly surprising that the pastoral role as such is also under question. In the past pastoral care has normally been seen as a function of the ordained priesthood or ministry. But when both traditional teaching and traditional priestly practices are under radical reappraisal, there is naturally also some uncertainty about whether ordination bestows any special competence in pas-toral care.

Other factors have added to this uncertainty. Since Freud discovered the phenomena of transference and counter-trans-ference in psychoanalysis, there has been a growing awareness of the emotional ambiguities in professional relationships. James Hillman[19] has expressed this succinctly in describing the interdependence of helper and helped:

> Just as the person who comes to me needs me for help, I need him to express my ability to give help. The helper and the needy, the social worker and the social case, the lost and the found, always go together.

Hillman goes on to point out that there is nothing wrong with such needs in the helper providing they do not become *demands* which force the other to satisfy them:

> A counsellor may need to instruct and educate, to teach what he knows, because it fulfils an essential part of him-self. . . . Yet he can hardly demand that each person coming to him, each visit, comes only for instruction. His need to teach may have to find other fulfilment, else it may become an unconscious demand on each person who comes to him.

Such observations have led to an ever-increasing emphasis on a self-critical awareness of the character of the helping rela-tionship itself.[20] In the field of theological education this has meant the emergence of a new type of training (now generally referred to as Clinical Pastoral Education) in which each individual student's pastoral encounters are subjected to intensive scrutiny both by an experienced supervisor and by a group of his fellow students.

In one sense there is nothing new in this emphasis on self-criticism. Manuals for confessors all stress the need for the confessor himself to attend confession, and handbooks in the Reformed tradition, like Baxter's *The Reformed Pastor*, devote many pages to the pastor's own need for self-examination and repentance. The difference, however, is the contemporary focus on the *emotional* characteristics of the helping relationship itself. The point is perhaps most clearly illustrated by the following quotation from Carl Rogers' essay: 'Some Hypotheses regarding the Facilitation of Personal Growth':[21]

> It has gradually been driven home to me that I cannot be of help . . . by means of any intellectual or training procedure. No approach which relies upon knowledge, upon training, upon the acceptance of something that is *taught*, is of any use. . . . The failure of any such approach through the intellect has forced me to recognize that change appears to come about through experience in a relationship.

Such a viewpoint tends to undercut professional authority based on knowledge or on designated role. Everything now hinges on the capacity of the helper to create a genuinely helpful relationship and all training and self-criticism must be directed toward that end. The counsellor is an authority only so far as he is able to help others to help themselves.

This approach has had a profound influence on contemporary understandings of pastoral care. The writings of Seward Hiltner[22] have effectively defined the terms of debate for the last three decades in categories concerned with the nature of the helping relationship. Deviations from Hiltner (like H. J. Clinebell's influential *Basic Types of Pastoral Counselling*) have offered alternative descriptions of the pastoral relationship, but have not questioned the basic assumption that it is in the relationship that the key to pastoral care and counselling is to be found. At the same time the revolutionary character of this approach has been somewhat obscured by the creation of a new type of religious professional, the 'pastoral counsellor', who may appear to be donning the mantle of the confessors and pastors of the past. But the stress on relationship rather than knowledge forces us to ask whether *any* person may not be a pastor to another simply from the depths of his or her own humanity, and whether the male, clerical dominance of the field from the past up to the present time may not be still obscuring many of its richest resources.

It is only by overcoming this third barrier between us and the tradition that we will be able to discover the true strength of a modern approach to pastoral care. Although it was often crude, and sometimes distorted the gospel into a form of legalism, the traditional approach of preacher and priest nevertheless consistently confronted the individual with the claims of his neighbour, of the world around him and of God. The care which was offered was related to fundamental issues of life and death, folly and wisdom, hope and despair. Is such confrontation and such richness of context inevitably linked with a formalized ecclesiastical role of pastor? There seems to be no obvious reason why this should be so. Can we not retain our emphasis on the mutuality of the helper and the helped, on the emotional dimensions of caring and on the priority of personal values within the helping relationship, without sacrificing the richness of meaning in the term 'pastoral'? In order to achieve this we need to find a new way of speaking of the transcendent element in pastoral care, one which starts from the character of the relationship itself. In the remainder of this chapter I shall be suggesting that the clue to such transcendent caring is to be found in the notion of 'integrity'.

PASTORAL CARE AS INTEGRITY

Let us suppose that we are a person seeking help and that our 'problem' (if that is the right word for it) will not fit neatly into the category of a physical illness or an emotional disturbance, though it may partly manifest itself in one or other of these. At the root of our difficulty is a sense of puzzlement, guilt or inadequacy. Perhaps we have suffered a particularly distressing bereavement, or have a feeling that our work is meaningless and unfulfilling, or suddenly find ourselves struck down by a life-threatening illness, or have to make a major decision of some kind and find ourselves incapable of making up our minds. We seek the help of another in our puzzlement and distress, hoping that his faith will somehow help us, his love restore our hope. What do we require from the other in order to be helped? Obviously we need the other to be warm and understanding and to be sincere in his offer of help. But has not the other more to offer to us than this? He too is a human being who must face desolation and vulnerability, despair and disillusionment, guilt and uncertainty. The person who helps another in a pastoral sense does so because through such human experiences he has developed (however provisionally, however inadequately) a certain *personal integrity*. All genuine care for those assailed by doubt and guilt proceeds from this integrity and without it no ecclesiastical role or counselling technique will be of help to others.

Integrity as Honesty and Steadfastness

When we speak of someone possessing 'integrity' we are trying to describe a quality of character for which the word 'honesty' may be too weak a synonym. To possess integrity is to be incapable of compromising that which we believe to be true. Perhaps then a word with a more old-fashioned ring – 'steadfastness' – may convey the richness of meaning better. To possess integrity is to have a kind of inner strength which prevents us from bending to the influence of what is thought expedient, or fashionable or calculated to win praise; it is to be consistent and utterly trustworthy because of a constancy of purpose. Yet the honesty conveyed by the word integrity is not to be confused with inflexibility and dogmatism, with the refusal to recognize error in oneself and the inability to perceive and respond to change in things around one. The person of integrity is first and foremost a critic of himself, of his own tendencies to self-deception and escape from reality, of his desire for a false inner security in place of the confrontation with truth which his integrity demands.

In his novel, *The Last Temptation*, Nikos Kazantzakis paints a vivid and passionately unorthodox picture of the struggles of Jesus to fulfill his mission. Jesus is portrayed as a maker of crosses who comes to realize that his destiny is to be crucified for the sins of the world. In one scene Judas is about to murder Jesus because of his participation in the execution of some zealot insurrectionists. Jesus offers no resistance when Judas draws his knife to kill him, and this completely unnerves Judas:

What kind of person is this? he asked himself. I can't understand. I wonder if it's the devil who's guiding him – or God? In either case, damn him! He leads him with a sure hand. He doesn't resist, and that is the greatest resistance. I can't slaughter lambs; men yes – but not lambs. 'You're a coward, you miserable wretch!' he burst out. . . . 'You're slapped on one cheek and you, what do you do, you right away turn the other. . . . A man can't touch you without feeling disgusted.'

'God can,' the son of Mary murmured tranquilly.[23]

It is this tranquillity that constitutes an important part of what I mean by speaking of pastoral care as integrity. It is a fearlessness, but a fearlessness won at great cost.

Another aspect of integrity is conveyed in George Bernard Shaw's portrayal of the courage of Joan of Arc. During her trial Joan has signed a confession denying her voices, but then she discovers to her horror that, although she will not now be burned at the stake, she will be sentenced to life imprisonment. She then defies her interrogators:

> You promised me my life; but you lied. I could do without my warhorse; I could drag about in a skirt; I could let the banners and the trumpets and the knights and soldiers pass me and leave me behind as they leave the other women, if only I could still hear the wind in the trees, the larks in the sunshine, the young lambs crying through the healthy frost, and the blessed, blessed church bells that send my angel voices floating to me on the wind. But without these things I cannot live; and by your wanting to take them away from me, or from any human creature, I know that your counsel is of the devil.[24]

Here integrity consists in loyalty to an inner truth which cannot be denied whatever the cost. For Joan, to be perpetually shut away from God's creation is a denial of herself and of God's love, which cannot be right. Thus burning at the stake, though she has thought her voices would never permit it, must, she realizes, be her inevitable choice.

Integrity as Wholeness and Oneness
Just as 'integrity' conveys an inner steadfastness and an outward honesty, so it equally suggests a wholeness upon which

13

such consistency is founded. C. G. Jung has discussed in many of his writings the problem which modern man faces in keeping in contact with the many different facets of his personality and of achieving a harmony or balance between them.[25] In an essay which examines personality crises in different stages of life, he describes the loss of parts of ourselves, incurred in the name of 'success':

> ... the achievements which society rewards are won at the cost of a diminution of personality. Many – far too many – aspects of life which should have been experienced lie in the lumber room among dusty memories. Sometimes, even, they are glowing coals under grey ashes.[26]

To possess integrity is to retain or to regain contact with the lost and repudiated aspects of ourselves, to clear the ashes from the glowing coals. But this is not achieved through the trivial glorification of 'self-realization' so common in contemporary popularized versions of psychotherapy. For, as Jung makes abundantly plain, no amount of introspection, self-discovery, seeking for the buried parts of our experience, can bring wholeness, if we make diversity and discovery our ultimate values. There is a mysterious centre to our being, hard to describe or discuss, yet indispensable to our integrity. Modern man's greatest problem is that he has lost contact with this centre and so experiences overwhelming feelings of disintegration.

W. B. Yeats' poem *The Second Coming* contains graphic images of this lostness:

> Turning and turning in the widening gyre
> The falcon cannot hear the falconer;
> Things fall apart; the centre cannot hold;
> Mere anarchy is loosed upon the world,
> The blood-dimmed tide is loosed, and everywhere
> The ceremony of innocence is drowned;
> The best lack all conviction, while the worst
> Are full of passionate intensity.[27]

What is this 'centre' with which we have lost contact? We can find attempts to speak of it in writings dealing with the contemplative aspects of Christian experience. Thomas Merton seeks to explain the meaning of the concept of 'the heart' used in traditional writings on prayer in the following terms:

It refers to the deepest psychological ground of one's personality, the inner sanctuary where self-awareness goes beyond analytical reflection, and opens out into metaphysical and theological confrontation with the Abyss of the unknown yet present – one who is 'more intimate to us than we are to ourselves'.[28]

Here we are uncovering a tension within the meaning of 'integrity' itself: on the one hand it expresses the determination of the individual to withstand external pressure, to be himself truly; and yet, when we seek for that which gives harmony and wholeness to the individual self, we find the *transcendence* of individuality. To be truly myself I must recognize that which is greater than me, yet which does not negate me. In losing myself, I find myself. In ceasing to take anxious pride in my individuality, I find a wholeness I never realized I possessed. Such paradoxes point to the richness of the concept of integrity as both steadfastness and oneness.

Steadfastness and Oneness in Pastoral Care
This preliminary sketch of the two aspects of integrity may provide some indication of the character of the relationship I believe pastoral care must aim to offer. It is out of the consistency and depth of the caring person's own character that help is given to another. Because he has known within himself the sense of failure and lostness which the other feels, the steadfastness and wholeness he offers is grounded in human reality. The carer and the cared for are not on two sides of a divide which must be bridged by some form of expertise on the part of the one who cares. Pastoral care is grounded in mutuality, not in expertise; it is possible because we share a common humanity with all the splendour and all the fallibility which that implies. If *I* can find some courage, hope and transcendence in the midst of life, then I can help my fellow men find that same wholeness; for I know that I am no better than they, no wiser, no more deserving of such fulfilment. Thus in speaking of pastoral care as an expression of integrity I am not intending to imply some kind of élitism in Christian care, as though only certain especially saintly people will have the qualities of character required. On the contrary, the sense of purpose and of transcendence which I have been describing comes to those who often least want or

expect it – those, who, like Kazantzakis' Jesus, are fearful and unwilling in the service of God; or who, like Bernard Shaw's Joan, find courage in their moments of greatest terror and weakness. In the last analysis there is no cleverness or accomplishment in pastoral care. It is no more (and no less) than sharing with another in the experience of grace, a surprising, unsought gift.

In the light of this, I believe it is essential for us to get away from the stress on *competence* which has dominated pastoral care since the emergence of a literature devoted to pastoral counselling.[29] Indeed expertise of any kind on the part of the provider of pastoral care must be viewed with great caution. We must remember that in describing pastoral care we are speaking of *the mediation of steadfastness and wholeness*, not the offering of advice at an intellectual level, nor the eliciting of insight at an emotional level. Such care, as I shall argue in greater detail later, depends to a great extent on the immediacy of our bodily presence not on counselling techniques. Words are often the enemy of care, for they seduce the carer and the cared for into playing verbal games, concealing still further the wholeness they might be able to seek together, if they did not fear the simplicity of silence.

Pastoral care as integrity must therefore be, first and foremost, that presence of one person with another which precedes all words. Pastoral care is embodied care, care incarnate.

THE WAY FORWARD

Where, then, do we go from here? How is the integrity which constitutes pastoral care to be described, discussed and implemented?

The first step in the rediscovery of pastoral care must consist in revitalizing the language in which it is described. If, as I have argued, the terminology of counselling expertise is inappropriate, what are the appropriate terms for conveying the unique character of such care? The problem seems to be that much of the traditional religious language, which might have served this purpose, has lost its communicative power. Its very familiarity has led us to misunderstand and neglect it. Yet in the Bible and in our religious traditions there reside

16

fundamental images of caring which could serve our purposes well if we could rediscover their richness. In the next chapter, 'The Power of Images', I shall discuss in general terms why such images are so important to an adequate understanding of pastoral care. (The reader who dislikes methodological discussions may choose to omit this chapter.) I shall then attempt to restore the vividness of three images of caring – the shepherd's courageous leadership (Chapter Three); the power of the wounded healer (Chapter Four); and the wisdom of the fool (Chapter Five). My aim in these chapters will be to rekindle an awareness of the resources we all possess for pastoral care, resources to be found as much in our weakness as in our strength.

The last section of the book (Chapters Six, Seven and Eight) suggests ways of implementing the caring which the images convey. Chapter Six tackles the issue of penitence referred to earlier in this chapter. A way towards wholeness *through* complexity is suggested by means of the embodiment of care. Chapter Seven returns to the theme of teaching and learning and discusses 'companionship on a journey' as a way of understanding how one person can help another towards faith. Finally, Chapter Eight suggests some 'paths of rediscovery' which might be followed by churches and theological schools in applying the ideas put forward in this book.

2

An Interlude: The Power Of Images

> Words strain,
> Crack and sometimes break, under the burden,
> Under the tension, slip, slide, perish,
> Decay with imprecision, will not stay in place,
> Will not stay still.
>
> T. S. Eliot, *Burnt Norton*[1]

The struggle to talk coherently about the nature of the relationship we call pastoral care derives from its fundamentally mysterious quality. In offering such care to another we begin to touch upon those ineffable experiences where life and death meet, where the values upon which human existence depends are under question, where the edges of our individual lives seem to merge with those of others. Thus we find ourselves dealing with areas of human endeavour which can be intuitively grasped but which resist logical analysis. I do not mean to imply that no rational account can be given of them, only that such accounts (say in the language of a philosophical or a theological system) tend to leave us with the feeling that something essential has been lost, that a vital aspect of the experience has dropped through the net of the conceptual system employed.

We therefore need to devise an appropriate method for discussing the nature of pastoral care – one which appeals as much to the imagination as to the intellect. Recent psychological research has suggested why this may be so. Logical and conceptual analysis is one way in which the mind may respond to the internal and external stimuli with which it is constantly bombarded. Since this way of ordering experience is highly adaptive for survival in a potentially hazardous environment, it tends to be given preference and to be regarded as the only correct way of describing 'reality'. But the mind simultaneously operates in a quite different mode on the endless flow of messages it receives. Rather than discriminating and naming, it responds to patterns and configurations, making associative connections not logical deductions. These two modes of understanding have been described by terms like 'linear' and 'lateral', 'converging' and 'diverging',[2] and it has been postulated that the difference corresponds to the different functions undertaken by the two hemispheres of the brain.[3] Undoubtedly this is a highly speculative area of psychological theory, and controversy about the validity of building an elaborate theory of knowledge on neurological evidence seems likely to continue indefinitely. But there is perhaps an increasing willingness to recognize that ways of describing experience which depend upon an intuitive awareness of interrelationships may be as valid a way of understanding the world as descriptions based upon the assumptions and methods of science.

IMAGES AND IMAGINATION

It is in the intuitive grasp of non-logical interrelationships that the image plays a unique role. The image is both the product of and the stimulus to the 'imagination', that is, to that aspect of our awareness which does not operate by the canons of linear rationality. Images are first and foremost sensuous in character, since they appeal directly to our responsiveness to visual stimuli and, to a lesser degree, to auditory, tactile, gustatory and olfactory stimuli. In its crudest form the image is no more than an impoverished reproduction of an original sense experience, which itself was much richer. Thus images are often dismissed as inadequate at best and deceptive at worst, because they provide a pale copy of reality. (See for example Plato's discussion of poetry and art in *The Republic*.)[4] But images can possess a power much greater than that of mere imitation. They are evocative of associations which may have been largely overlooked in the original experience.

Consider, for example, the difference between a holiday snapshot of a country scene and a painting of the same scene by a great artist. The former may evoke associations, but only of a quite personal kind for those who were present on the holiday, and it is unlikely that the snapshot will stimulate any new awareness of that experience. But the painting has the power to evoke associations of a deeper and more universal kind. The painting reveals the original scene in a different way from a simple reproduction; it 'opens the eyes' of the person able to respond to it to features of light, shape and colour which he might otherwise miss; and it creates responses in him which he can describe only with the vaguest of words, like 'beauty' or 'serenity' or 'depth'. Moreover, the painting has the power to evoke such responses in those who have never seen the original scene which it portrays.

It is this transcendence of the particular, broadening of awareness and evocation of associations that make the image of great potential value in portraying the elusive and mysterious character of caring for others.[5] We might choose to use the terminology of Paul Tillich at this point and suggest that such images have become *symbols* which 'participate in the reality toward which they point' and which are, therefore, of much greater significance than simple copies or imitations of the eternal form of things.[6] Tillich's account is also helpful in reminding us that symbols 'grow and die',[7] a point to which we shall return when discussing specific images for pastoral care. But although the notion of 'symbol' helps to identify the class of images in which I am interested, I wish to keep the discussion centred on concrete *images* of caring, rather than on the somewhat more abstract symbols which such images may become. There is a certain immediacy, vividness and spontaneity in images, which seem to me important when we are trying to understand the human dimensions of care.

Of course we can also lose our way in images because of their free flowing character. We can try to shape the world according to our 'vain imaginings', using the imagination as an escape from, rather than a response to, the mystery of the world as we experience it. Martin Buber describes this destructive aspect of imagination well in his account of the Fall and the consequent 'knowledge of good and evil':

In the swirling space of images through which (man) strays, each and every thing entices to be made incarnate by him . . . it all becomes reality, though no longer divine but his,

his capriciously constructed, indestinate reality, his violence, which overcomes him, his handiwork and fate.[8]

Yet we need not renounce imagination because of its potentially chaotic and deceptive character. Imagination need not result in an unbridled and arbitrary creation of our own fantasy world. There is also the *responsive* imagination, which, rather than destroying man with his own handiwork, takes him beyond himself to encounter with fellow man and with God. Later in the same essay, Buber suggests that man's urge for creation if combined with the urge for union with God will no longer lead him astray:

> To unite the two urges implies: to equip the absolute potency of passion with the one direction that renders it capable of great love and great service. Thus and not otherwise can man become whole.[9]

A similarly positive view of the power of the imagination has been taken by William F. Lynch. Lynch believes that the way to insight is always the 'narrow way' through 'the finite, the limited, the definite, omitting none of it lest we omit some of the potencies of being-in-the-flesh'.[10] Lynch contrasts this approach with four other possible attitudes which may be adopted to the imagination's relationship with the finite: (1) The use of the finite as a 'jumping off point' for a detached, mystical vision; (2) The use of the finite as a way of rebounding into the self in order to produce a heightened state of affectivity ('psychologism'); (3) A 'two worlds' view, drawing a radical contrast between the finite on the one hand and the heavenly or infinite on the other; (4) A 'facers of facts' approach which denies that there is anything other than the finite and insists that we must courageously accept its absurdity and limitation. Against these views Lynch reiterates his own hopes for the imagination:

> The ideal solution would be that the world should 'signify' without becoming less actual in so doing. Our hope must be to discover such symbols as can make the imagination *rise* indeed, and yet keep all the tang and density of that actuality into which the imagination *descends*.[11]

Lynch's 'ideal solution' and the alternatives with which he contrasts it are of central importance for the subsequent argument in this book. We can see how the second alternative approach ('psychologism') has tended to dominate recent pastoral counselling literature, with its frequent use of 'need satisfaction', 'self actualization' or 'personal growth' as the goals of counselling.[12] The critics of this literature, on the other hand, have often attacked it on the basis of a 'two worlds' approach, denying the imaginative capacities of the individual and insisting on the 'objective' character of God's Word.[13] My concern is to discuss pastoral care from the perspective of actual human experience, but in so doing to uncover images which remind us of the transcendent dimension of this experience. My assumption is that there are available to us images of sufficient power to convey an intuitive understanding of the care which is required of us in pastoral relationships. I am trying (with what success remains to be seen) to take Lynch's 'narrow road' through the finite to the transcendent.

THE DISTORTED IMAGE

At this point we are confronted by a fresh difficulty. We have already noticed that Tillich spoke of symbols 'growing and dying'. A similar fate befalls images. When first used they enliven our understanding by their vividness and often unexpected associations. But when an image is enshrined in spoken and written words it soon begins to become blurred and distorted, and perhaps to fade away altogether. Take, for example, the idiomatic phrase, 'By and large'. How many users of it realize that it contains an image of sailing ships, which can be full-sailed in the wind ('large') or barely catching it ('by') or somewhere in-between ('by and large')? Countless other examples could be taken of the fading away of images. A notable one is the almost totally unconscious use of military imagery in speaking of medical treatment. 'Campaigns' are mounted against diseases, which are seen to be 'invading' the body and therefore must be 'combated'. If the disease has not been 'wiped out' by the treatment of choice, it must be 'attacked' by different methods until it is finally 'defeated'.[14] In this example, we see the problems created by an image which has blurred to the point where it is no longer really noticed. The imagery makes the patient into an inert battlefield across which the rival forces of treatment and disease relentlessly march. Now that we understand something of the psycho-somatic nature of illness, such imagery is clearly inadequate, but, because it has become hackneyed and familiar, the need to find more adequate language never becomes sufficiently pressing to lead to its replacement. A further example of both blurring and distortion may be found in the modern understanding of the New Testament affirmation: 'Jesus Christ is Lord'. At the time of its formulation both 'Christ' and 'Lord' had vivid associations with Jewish messianic hopes and with the religions and the power politics of the Gentile world. Not only have these original images faded, but centuries of Christian piety have created entirely new associations, largely obscuring the communal and political references of the originals.

We are now in a position to see why the restoration of the images of pastoral care is such a major task. It is immediately obvious that both blurring and distortion have taken place in the central image of 'shepherding' from which the phrase 'pastoral care' derives. As we shall see later (Chapter Three), this was a powerful image in biblical times, creating immediate associations with the sights and sounds of everyday life in Palestine. But what relevance can such a rural image have for the majority of people in Western society today, or for urban communities elsewhere in the world? Moreover, the image has been badly distorted by the literature and art of much sentimental piety. The 'Good Shepherd' of many religious paintings is a somewhat effete and delicate figure, far removed from the hardiness and physical courage of the original. But perhaps the major problem with the imagery of shepherding is that it seems to encourage an alien and demeaning form of paternalism: the sheep are errant, feckless, easily led astray; the shepherd is dedicated, powerful and always knows what is best for the sheep. The impression of an all-embracing, paternalistic style of care has been increased by the fusing of the image of shepherd (pastor) with the image of father (priest). 'Pastoral care' has thereby come to mean 'soul-care' by a wise and fatherly figure whose superior spiritual insight and moral rectitude equips him to lead his 'flock' to safety. Such a view is quite incompatible with the notion of mutuality in caring, which, I have argued

(Chapter One above), must form part of a contemporary understanding of pastoral care.

The difficulties which these blurrings, distortions and added associations create for a contemporary understanding of pastoral care are far from easy to overcome. Because images operate at a non-rational level primarily, they cannot be altered by a simple process of argument. A radical solution would be to abandon the term 'pastoral' altogether and try to find an alternative word to describe the kind of care we have in mind. Yet, even if this could succeed, it may not be entirely necessary. On the one hand, the shepherd image has faded to such an extent that the word 'pastoral' is largely empty – a blank cheque, as it were, on which we may now write the value we wish to give to care. On the other hand, there are aspects of the original imagery which seem well worth restoring, since they give concrete expression to the steadfastness and wholeness which constitutes pastoral care as integrity.

RESTORING THE IMAGES

In the light of what I have said, the first priority in the pages which follow will be a re-examination of the image of the shepherd as it occurs in the Old and New Testaments. We shall see that it is undeniably a portrayal of leadership, but the *quality* of that leadership is of prime importance. The shepherd's courage gives a particular colouring to our understanding of care. Numerous other images could be added to that of the shepherd in order to enrich the meaning of care.[15] However, two central paradoxes of the Christian gospel seem closest to the heart of the matter. These are the power of vulnerability and the wisdom of folly. Each has a vivid image attached to it: the wounded healer and the clown or fool. These images provide a corrective to the excessively heroic and authoritarian associations which 'shepherd' can attract to itself, and help to form a link with our own stumbling efforts to care for others.

Taken together, these three images will be used to describe that peculiar quality of care which pastoral relationships can provide. But it must be added that such images are only the beginnings of what must be a continuing effort of the imagination. As we explore the topics of penitence and of faith (Chapters Six and Seven) fresh images will appear – images of sexuality and of bodily decay, of friendship and of repose, of journeying and of mortal combat; and, if they are effective, these images should in turn evoke fresh imaginative associations. There cannot be, and should not be, an end to our image work, for, what we are describing is not a world of abstract ideas, but the mysterious depths of human experience in its response to a living God.

3

The Shepherd's Courage

Love is the greatest of all risks
  to give myself to you
  do I dare . . . do I dare
leap into the cool, swirling, living waters
  of loving fidelity?

Jean Vanier, *Tears of Silence*[1]

In order to revitalize the imagery of pastoral care we must restore to it a much neglected quality – courage. Anyone who has entered into the darkness of another's pain, loss or bewilderment and who has done so without the defences of a detached professionalism will know the feeling of wanting to escape, of wishing they had not become involved. Caring is costly, unsettling, even distasteful at times. The valley of deep shadows in an other person's life frightens us too, and we lack the courage and constancy to enter it. One of the most vivid aspects of the biblical image of shepherding (from which the term 'pastoral' derives) is such courage, courage to the point of risking one's own life. Thus young David, anxious to convince Saul that he is capable of fighting Goliath, uses as a testimonial his experiences as a shepherd boy:

> 'Your Majesty', David said, 'I take care of my father's sheep. Whenever a lion or a bear carries off a lamb, I go after it, attack it, and rescue the lamb. And if the lion or bear turns on me, I grab it by the throat and beat it to death. . . . The Lord saved me from lions and bears; he will save me from this Philistine.' (1 Sam. 17: 34–7 TEV)

It is this element of courage based on trust in God which seems most obviously neglected in modern accounts of pastoral relationships. But there are also other features of the

26

shepherd's character – tenderness, skill in leadership, concern for wholesomeness – making up a rich picture of what it means to care. In order to recover these elements it is necessary to summarize the usage of the image in the Old and New Testaments, and then consider its relevance for a contemporary understanding of pastoral care.

Biblical Images of Shepherding
Shepherding in the climatic conditions of Palestine was (and is) a demanding and, at times, hazardous occupation. During the long dry season it was necessary to move the flocks over considerable distances in search of good pastures; suitable resting places and watering places had to be found; and danger lurked in the shadows of valleys in the form of robbers and wild beasts – as David's description so graphically demonstrates. The shepherd was with his flock day and night, often in remote places far from home, and he had to be skilled in keeping the flock together, in finding wanderers and stragglers, in recognizing the ailments of his sheep and knowing how to cure them, and in ensuring the safety of the vulnerable members of the flock.

We can see at once that there is a mixture of tenderness and toughness in the character of the shepherd. His unsettled and dangerous life makes him a slightly ambiguous figure – more perhaps like the cowboy of the 'Wild West' than the modern shepherd in a settled farming community. The shepherd, like the cowboy, may be a hired man in a dangerous job, who cannot always be relied upon (John 10: 11ff), especially since he wanders from place to place. Thus in Rabbinic writings shepherds are viewed with considerable suspicion. They are accused of handling stolen goods and trespassing on other people's pastureland, and (in common with publicans and tax gatherers) are not permitted to hold judicial office or give evidence in court.[2]

Tenderness, Skill and Self-Sacrifice
In the Old Testament, however, the disreputable aspect of the image is rarely if ever present. The positive attributes of the good shepherd are given prominence and used to express the loving leadership of God and of his promised Messiah. The shepherd leads, guides, nurtures, heals, seeks out the lost, brings the scattered flock back together and protects it

from harm. The image occurs most frequently in the Psalms and in the Exilic prophecies of Jeremiah, Ezekiel and Deutero-Isaiah.[3] Perhaps it is nowhere more vivid as an image of tenderness and hope than in Isaiah 40:

> He will feed his flock like a shepherd,
>   he will gather the lambs in his arms,
>   he will carry them in his bosom,
>   And gently lead those that are with young.
>
> (Isa. 40: 11 RSV)

The skill of the shepherd and his concern for wholesomeness are portrayed in Ezekiel 34:

> I will look for those that are lost, bring back those that wander off, bandage those that are hurt, and heal those that are sick.
>
> (Ezek. 34: 16 TEV)

The same healing skills are described in the familiar opening verses of Psalm 23:

> He lets me rest in fields of green grass and leads me to quiet pools of fresh water
> He gives me new strength
> He guides me in the right paths,
> as he has promised.
>
> (Ps. 23: 2f TEV)

The idea that the shepherd's care for the sheep can even lead to his own death finds expression in Zechariah's accounts of the messianic shepherd whose death leads to a purification of the people (Zech. 11:4; 12:10; 13:7–9):

> They will look at the one whom they stabbed to death, and they will mourn for him like those who mourn for an only child.
>
> (Zech. 12: 10 TEV)

The Care of the Despised
In the New Testament we find the shepherd motif throughout the accounts of Jesus' birth, ministry, death, resurrection and final triumph. In the Lucan nativity story, it is shepherds who are called to witness the Messiah's birth. They are sent by the angels to an animal stall, whose location they clearly

already know, perhaps because they used it for their own flocks.[4] The choice of shepherds – that rough and perhaps untrustworthy group – as first witnesses of Jesus' birth accords well with Luke's stress on the humility of the nativity:

> He has brought down mighty kings from their thrones and lifted up the lowly.
>
> (Luke 1: 52 TEV)

Jesus uses the shepherd image in his teaching to express God's strenuous and often surprising concern for those who have gone astray. (Mat. 18: 12–14 and par.) It is perhaps significant that in Luke's version of the parable of the lost sheep the context is the accusation by the scribes and Pharisees that Jesus eats with outcasts (Luke 15: 4–7). In response, Jesus uses the care and concern of the distrusted shepherd as a paradigm for God's love, as elsewhere (Luke 10: 30–37) he uses the loving actions of the despised Samaritan. The death of Jesus – that final act of caring love – is referred to in terms which recall the messianic Shepherd of the Old Testament prophecies. In John 10 Jesus claims the title, Good Shepherd, because (unlike the hireling) Jesus is willing to die for the sheep. In the Synoptic Gospels (Mark 14: 27f and par.) Jesus quotes Zechariah's prophecy of the smitten shepherd in order to speak of his death, the sheeplike panic of his disciples and his shepherding of them (Eastern fashion) by leading the way to Galilee after his resurrection.[5] The same imagery of sacrifice and leadership is used in Revelation to describe the triumph of the Christian martyrs who are led to safety by him who is both sacrificial lamb and shepherd:

> The lamb, who is in the centre of the throne, will be their shepherd, and he will guide them to springs of life-giving water.
>
> (Rev. 7: 17a TEV)

In similar terms the benediction at the end of Hebrews accords Jesus the title Great Shepherd, because of his sacrificial death (Heb. 13:20), just as earlier (2:10) he is called the 'trail blazer' (*archegon*) to salvation.

Leadership
In this widespread use of the shepherd image in the Bible we see an interesting picture emerging. The shepherd is undoubt-

edly a leader – a strong and courageous figure at the head of his flock. But his leadership has a very special quality. His concern is entirely focused on those entrusted to his care, even to the point of surrendering his own life. Thus his leadership is expressed in great compassion, sensitivity to need and a knowledge of what is life-sustaining and wholesome. It is an image linked to the feel of strong supporting arms, to the taste of cool refreshing water and to the sensation of receiving truly strengthening nourishment. It is a leadership of real physical involvement, basic and simple, leadership even when one's own blood is spilled and one's own body broken.

In view of its leadership associations it is perhaps not surprising that shepherd or 'pastor' became a term to describe the leader of a Christian congregation. But in fact its use in this way is relatively unusual in the New Testament.[6] Most of the references consist of the use of the verb 'to shepherd' (*poimainein*), to describe the duties of the elders (*presbuteroi*) or overseers (*episcopoi*) of the new Christian congregations. A good example can be found in 1 Peter:

> I appeal to you to be shepherds of the flock (*poimanate to poimnion*) that God gave you and to take care of it willingly as God wants you to and not unwillingly. Do your work, not for mere pay, but from a real desire to serve. Do not try to rule over those who have been put in your care, but be examples to the flock.
>
> (1 Peter 5:2f TEV)

(Cf. Paul's words to the elders at Ephesus: Acts 20:28)

The *title* 'Pastor' (*poimen*) is used only once in the New Testament to describe a church official (Eph. 4:11). The context is a list of gifts given by God to 'build up the body of Christ' and here 'pastors and teachers' are regarded as having a separate function from 'apostles, prophets and evangelists'. One can see how such a 'pastoral' function became necessary as the young churches settled into an established life following the initial evangelization which established them. The task of the pastor-teacher was one of ensuring continuity of life and doctrine, as years and generations passed. He was there to remind people of the meaning and practical implications of the gospel which led them into the Christian community in the first place.

It is unfortunate, however, that this pastoral teaching office (often combined with the office of leader of worship) quickly tended to absorb within itself the whole meaning of 'pastoral'. It becomes assumed that *this* leadership is the *only* leadership referred to when we speak of pastoral care. Nothing could be farther from the truth. The primary reference of the shepherd image is to Jesus' self-sacrificial love, which seeks a response from *every* one of his followers. Leaders and teachers of congregations have no special prerogatives in this central meaning of shepherding. We must learn to speak of the *pastorhood of all believers* and to explore the idea that *each* person has a call to lead in that special way characteristic of the Good Shepherd.

In exploring this use of shepherding I shall first examine a modern account of pastoral care given in the writings of the American pastoral theologian, Seward Hiltner. A critique of this account will lead me to suggest some richer uses of the shepherding imagery to describe our call to be loving leaders.

A MODERN USE OF 'SHEPHERDING'

The importance of Seward Hiltner for contemporary developments in pastoral care and pastoral counselling theory can hardly be overestimated. His books, notably *Pastoral Counseling*, *Preface to Pastoral Theology* and *The Christian Shepherd*, have set the terms of reference for discussion of pastoral issues for the past two decades in the U.S.A. and have widely influenced writers in other countries. His work marks the beginning of a new academic rigour in pastoral theology, one which takes theory in the 'secular' sciences of man seriously. But perhaps Hiltner's most important contribution has been to free the term 'pastoral' from its association with the title 'pastor', which itself has become simply a synonym for 'minister' or 'leader of a congregation'. It is evident from nineteenth-century textbooks on 'pastoral theology' that, because of this association, 'pastoral' had come to mean little more than 'what the minister does', whether this was teaching, preaching or visiting the sick.[7] Other textbooks identified a specific area of ministerial work – 'poimenics' – which was to take its place

alongside homiletics, catechetics, etc.[8] In place of such functional and role-related definitions Hiltner argued that we
must understand 'pastoral' to be a *perspective* from which all
activities of church and ministry may be viewed, a perspective
based on 'the shepherd's attitude of tender and solicitious
concern'. In certain activities of church and ministry this
perspective may be the dominant one; in others it may give
place to other concerns (for example, the need to communi-
cate the gospel or to organize the fellowship), but it should
never be wholly absent, since the shepherding attitude is an
essential aspect of Christian faith.

The reorientation which Hiltner offers is a useful one in
restoring some of the unique qualities of shepherding, but it
also has some serious flaws. In the first place, Hiltner appears
to remain trapped in an uncritical view of the nature of the
Church and the purpose of its ministry. His writings still
assume a minister-dominated approach to pastoral care[9] and
the pastoral theology which he constructs on the basis of
reflection on current 'operations' of the Church is insulated
from theological critique by the nature of its purely practical
starting point.[10] Another, and (for our purposes) fatal flaw in
Hiltner's account of 'the shepherding perspective' is that it is
remarkably flat and uninteresting. We look in vain for the
drama and vividness of the biblical imagery in his descriptions
of pastoral care, pastoral counselling and pastoral theology.
Instead we find a fondness for the terminology of non-directive or client-centred counselling. Thus, in *The Christian
Shepherd* he describes the 'basic principles of shepherding' as
concern, acceptance, clarification, judgement, humility and
self-understanding.[11] No doubt these are admirable qualities,
but their connection with the shepherd image seems tangen-
tial at best. Moreover the biblical references given in the
various explanations of the origins of the shepherd motif are
remarkably selective. The parables of the lost sheep and of
the good Samaritan are used to illustrate the meaning of care
and concern,[12] but the Old Testament themes of consolation
and hope are not mentioned nor is the powerfully sacrificial
element in the New Testament image. Jesus as the Great
Shepherd of the Hebrews benediction is mentioned in one
sentence, but nothing is said of the messianic hopes with
which the New Testament writers viewed Jesus as shepherd.
We are forced to conclude that in Hiltner the image is little

more than a cipher which gives a religious appearance to statements about care derived from quite other sources, notably the faith-statements of Rogerian counselling theory. A consequence of this is that Hiltner's use of shepherding offers little or no illumination into how we can be shepherds to one another on that dangerous route which results from following Jesus. The encouragement to be non-directive counsellors is a less than adequate account of the risks entailed!

COURAGE AND INTEGRITY IN PASTORAL CARE

Unhelped by Hiltner's 'tender and solicitous concern' we are forced to return to a tougher aspect of 'the shepherding perspective' – courage. Yet this at once seems to create a problem. The 'tough man' image has been exploited to such an extent in fiction, films and television programmes that we tend to equate courage with violence and physical strength. In speaking of courage in pastoral care, how can we escape from the idea that some people are 'natural leaders' and somehow superior to others in so being? The corrective must come from the constant reminders in the Old and New Testaments that God reveals to man what true shepherding is and saves him from the exploitation and neglect of false shepherds and untrustworthy hirelings. Thus it is in the stead-fast love of God incarnate in Jesus that we see the shepherd's courage, not in the power and strength of earthly leaders. The courage of Jesus has a quality to it that is both strong and gentle. Above all, it is a courage *for others*, not a courage for his own defence or aggrandizement. We shall look briefly at some aspects of this courage as they were shown in his life.

1. There is courage in the words of Jesus. On many occasions Jesus is put to the test by his opponents: Should we render tribute to Caesar? By what authority do you do this? Who has sinned, this man or his parents? Is it lawful to heal on the Sabbath? Which is the greatest commandment? Why do you eat with taxgatherers and sinners? Are you the Messiah, the King of the Jews? The answers of Jesus are both calm and fearless. They spring from an inner strength which comes from his oneness with his Father and his certainty that no law and no earthly power can prevail against love.[13]

2. There is courage in the actions of Jesus. He touches

33

lepers and speaks to the possessed. He confronts an angry crowd, preventing a stoning by his intervention. He eats with quislings and the socially outcast and joyfully accepts the tears and kisses of a prostitute. He rides into Jerusalem in a public procession, knowing that his enemies are watching his every move. He boldly enters the temple courts and drives out the money-makers. He casts aside all dignity, humbly washing the feet of his friends. He shares bread with the man who will betray him and enters the garden to receive the kiss which leads to arrest, punishment and death.

3. There is courage in the sufferings of Jesus. He willingly shares the burden of the poor, the homeless and the sick. He rejects the comforts of family and possessions, finding mother and brothers in those who will hear him. He accepts the friendship of men who misunderstand, neglect and deny him. He overcomes the temptations of supernatural power, and in his agony in Gethsemane finds a way to bend his fear and sorrow to God's will. He endures taunts, flogging and a slow death in dereliction, because he knows it is the way that love requires. In his dying moments he seeks only forgiveness for his executioners and the fulfilment of God's will.

Such is the courage of the Good Shepherd who lays down his life for the sheep. It is the courage of integrity, of an inner wholeness, of a oneness with God and with man and of a constant, invincible love. In such a context our own attempts to care for others seem hopelessly weak and inadequate. There is a clear limit to the suffering most of us would be willing to endure for the sake of others, especially those with whom we have no ties of family or of close affection. We also lack courage in action and in words, mainly because there is no sure centre to our being. We lean desperately on the good will and praise of others or on the reassurance of possessions and of social standing, because we have no trust in our own worth without these external validations. Since we lack an inner wholeness we do not have the grace to speak to others with both tenderness and strength. It matters too much to us whether the other is pleased and too little whether we speak the truth as best we see it. We cannot be shepherds so long as comfort is our main concern and so long as the roads through the wilderness are too lonely and too dangerous for us.

Thus, far from giving us a simple paradigm for our caring

concern, the image of the shepherd seems merely to reveal our inadequacies. If it is the sacrificial love of Jesus that the pastoral relationship demands of us, we know before we begin that the goal is unattainable. Yet perhaps it is no bad thing that the central image in pastoral care, when properly appreciated, has this humbling effect. It must surely finally dispose of all self-confident 'management models' for pastoral care. There is no way of organizing our lives and the lives of others to *ensure* that the lost are found, that the weak are protected, that pastures are truly wholesome, that there is pure, clear water. Perhaps in a literal sense we can organize for physical needs (though the starvation and violence throughout the world show little promise of that), but the green pastures and still waters of total human wellbeing are still harder to find, and for each person the way is unique. If pastoral care begins to depend on some technique which can be easily taught and implemented, then we can be sure that it has become something else – a method of psychological adjustment to society perhaps, or a way of increasing church membership, or a system of spiritual consolation against the harsh realities of the world.

How then can we understand our task as 'loving leaders', as under-shepherds of the Great Shepherd? The answer lies in holding on to the eschatological element in all our attempts to describe pastoral care. The way of Jesus leads across stony ground, through dark valleys to the living water. The peace and fulfilment given in Jesus is *both* in our midst *and* yet to come. To suggest that personal wellbeing and the wholeness of life on earth among men are easily within our grasp is to obscure with a facile optimism the judgement and hope in the message of Jesus; but to dismiss as futile all human efforts to love and care and to lead others to wholesomeness is to deny with a false pessimism the incarnate nature of God's love. Somewhere in the tension between these two extremes there lies the possibility for pastoral care. This possibility will come to different people at different moments. Sometimes it will be right for me to lead, sometimes gratefully to accept the leadership of another. No single human being possesses the competence, the strength or the vision to arrogate to himself the role of the Good Shepherd. But when it is our place to lead the way for others there are two signs that our shepherding is true leadership. The first is that those who follow our lead

35

find rest and health, not some narrowing, overburdening or destruction of themselves. (Much shepherding in the name of religion has such unwholesome results.)[14] The second sign is that true leadership is costly and dangerous. We cannot lead without risking ourselves. Indeed (as we shall see in the next chapter) it is most often out of our wounds that we bring wholeness to others. When we experience this second sign, the sign of the wounded healer, we also realize how little we can give of pastoral care and how much we ourselves need it.

4

The Wounded Healer

Wounded oysters build out of gory wounds
a pearl. And create within the gap of pain
a jewel.
May we be so wise.

Richard Shannon,
The Peacock and the Phoenix[1]

As we seek more deeply for those resources of help and guidance which we have to offer others in pastoral care we find them in a surprising place – in our vulnerability. It is natural for us to suppose that we must help out of our strength. Indeed all *professional* intervention in the lives of others depends upon a certain strength or superiority.[2] The professional helper has a particular form of knowledge and skill which he puts at the disposal of his client. He claims expertise, and on the basis of such he becomes an authorized or registered helper of others. Pastoral care, however, is not correctly understood if it is viewed within the framework of professionalism.[3] As I have already argued (see Chapter One), pastoral care is a relationship founded upon the integrity of the individual. Such a relationship does not depend primarily upon the acquisition of knowledge or the development of skill. Rather it depends upon a caring attitude towards others which comes from our own experience of pain, fear and loss and our own release from their deadening grip.

Here we can begin to see the importance of the second image of care, the Wounded Healer. This image is central to the Christian understanding of the significance of Jesus' death:

Through him God chose to reconcile the whole universe to

himself, making peace through the shedding of his blood upon the cross – to reconcile all things, whether on earth or in heaven through him alone.

(Col. 1:20 NEB)

Christ, the Wounded Healer, restores the fractured relationships between God, man and the whole universe. We do a grave injustice to the incarnate love of God if we try to understand the suffering and death of Jesus merely as some kind of legal transaction paying the 'penalty' for man's sin in a distanced, 'objective' way. Jesus' wounds, in life and in death, are the expressions of his openness to our suffering. He suffered because of his love: his sufferings are the stigmata of his care for us and for the whole world estranged from God. Such wounded love has a healing power because it is enfleshed love, entering into human weakness, feeling our pain, standing beside us in our dereliction:

> The other gods were strong but
>   Thou wast weak;
> They rode, but Thou didst stagger
>   to a throne.
> But to our wounds only God's
>   wounds can speak,
> And not a god has wounds but
>   Thou alone.[4]

Jürgen Moltmann stresses this total involvement by speaking of the 'human God', the 'crucified God':

> Anyone who suffers without cause first thinks that he has been forsaken by God. God seems to him to be the mysterious, incomprehensible God who destroys the good fortune that he gave. But anyone who cries out to God in his suffering echoes the death-cry of the dying Christ, the Son of God. In that case God is not just a hidden someone set over against him, to whom he cries, but in a profound sense the human God, who cries with him and intercedes for him with his cross, where man in his torment is dumb.[5]

So we may understand the humbling of Christ Jesus (Phil. 2:8), the stripes of the Suffering Servant (Isa. 53:5), the life-ransom of the Son of Man (Mat. 20:28) as ways of healing, because it is in this utter weakness that the power of God is

38

found. Such is the vividness of the original image of the Wounded Healer that (in the words of Dame Julian of Norwich) it is both 'horrifying and dreadful, sweet and lovely'[6]. The sheer physical horror of the mocking, flogging and crucifixion of Jesus takes us into the depths of human degradation and cruelty, yet in deepest darkness we find the flame of love. It is this intertwining of suffering and strength which allows Paul to see hope and healing coming directly from his own suffering and from the suffering of the Corinthian Christians to whom he writes:

> Just as we have a share in Christ's many sufferings, so also through Christ we share in God's great help. If we suffer, it is for your help and salvation; if we are helped, then you too are helped and given the strength to endure with patience the same sufferings that we also endure. (2 Cor. 1:5f TEV)

How then may the image of the Wounded Healer help us to understand the nature of pastoral care today? I shall consider first the associations which the language of wounds evokes and then discuss the practical implications of a care which derives from such vulnerability.

THE LANGUAGE OF WOUNDS

A wound is an opening in the walls of our body, a breaking of the barrier between us and the world around us. James Hillman points out that such an opening is 'a passage through which we may become infected and also through which we affect others'.[7] Naturally, then, we view wounds with distaste and alarm. The sight of blood and of gaping flesh creates sensations of nausea and fear in us, because it warns of pain, permanent damage to the body and the spread of infection. Our instinct for self-preservation leads us to avoid wounds whenever possible and, when they are sustained, to seek immediate remedy.

Yet paradoxically our fear and nausea would be much greater if we encountered a body which could not bleed, could not be wounded. Blood is a sign of life for us and the softness of skin and flesh reveals humanity. (Hence the poignancy of Shylock the Jew's question: 'If you prick us, do we not

39

bleed. . . . If you poison us, do we not die?')[8] This means that open wounds and flowing blood evoke other associations: the break in the body's walls can bring the wounded person closer to us. We respond to his vulnerability, seeing before us 'a fellow-creature in pain'.[9] Thus blood and wounds have important positive effects in creating a sense of community. The opening in the body is a channel of communication from one isolated individual to another; the hazardous outflowing of blood an ultimate risking of the self for others. These communal aspects are evident both in the ritual sacrifices of the Jewish temple cult and in the Christian Eucharist: blood becomes the seal of reconciliation between man and man and between man and God.

Moreover, as the words of the Eucharist remind us, a wounded body and flowing blood speak also of death, the inevitable concomitant of vulnerability: 'every time you eat this bread and drink from this cup you proclaim the Lord's death until he comes' (1 Cor. 11:26 TEV). Death is the final proof of our humanity. Without it we would be different beings, knowing nothing of the light and shadow of human life.

The poet, Richard Shannon, conveys the importance of death to our appreciation of the beauty of life by a comparison of the living flower with the plastic flower:

> How exquisite and how perfect is the living flower which knows both birth and dying: while the plastic flower which lasts a thousand years is ever brutal in its changelessness. The softness of one and the hardness of the other. It is vulnerability that makes one open and beautiful. And surely without death there is no vulnerability.[10]

Surprisingly, then, wounds, which seem at first frightening and nauseating, can also be 'open and beautiful'. For, wounds reveal that fine boundary between living and dying, which makes human life so precious and so revered. In the sombre cadences of Ecclesiastes the beauty of such fragility is captured in a flow of metaphors:

> The silver chain will snap, and the golden lamp will fall and break; the rope at the well will break, and the water jar will be shattered. Our bodies will return to the dust of

the earth, and the breath of life will go back to God, who gave it to us.

(Eccles. 12:6f TEV)

Yet we must beware of becoming morbidly, even sentimentally, preoccupied with blood, wounds and death, as though they of themselves were sources of healing. The mere fact of experiencing wounds does not restore health. The pain of wounds can demean and destroy people, closing them off from hope in an in-turned and seemingly endless agony. Death is not only the token of our humanity. It is also an affront to our humanity, bringing fear, anger and loneliness in its wake.[11] Wounds, and the vulnerability which they represent, lead to healing *only* when they have been uncovered and dealt with; otherwise they are festering sores which destroy our health and the health of those with whom we deal. The practical consequence for the person who would help others is clear: 'I will be forced to pay attention to my own sufferings and needs, if I am to be of service to anyone else' (Hillman).[12]

Two incidents from the life of Jesus illustrate this point well: when a woman anoints Jesus with precious ointment, he rejects the protests of his disciples that such a costly gift could be better used to raise money for the poor: his is the greater need, for his death is impending and this act acknowledges in a sensitive way the suffering which is to come. So this act of loving has an enduring significance, a ministering to the dying Wounded One (Mat. 26:6–13). Similarly, when Jesus goes to pray in the Garden of Gethsemane, overwhelmed by sorrow and longing for release from the darkening future, he asks for support from his friends: 'The sorrow in my heart is so great that it almost crushes me. Stay here and keep watch with me' (Mat. 26:38 TEV). He knows his need well. He is no passionless demi-god exempt from the terror of torture and death. As it turns out, his disciples fail to respond to his need and he must face the darkness, interceding alone with his Father. But he has not hidden from his fear, and when he takes the cup of sorrow it is with the tranquillity of one who has faced his own terrible destiny.

Thus the Wounded Healer gains his power by acknowledging his weakness and by finding God's healing force at the moment of deepest despair. There is no shortcut to such

41

healing, no hope without fear, no resurrection without the tomb's deep darkness. We must now see how, by acknowledging our wounds and facing our finitude, we too, in a small way, can be healers of others.

THE WOUND'S HEALING

We have seen that the authority with which we offer help to others derives from our own acquaintance with grief. Conversely, if we have always sheltered ourselves from experiences of pain in our own lives, the consolation we offer will be empty. This does not imply that we can help another person only if we ourselves have had precisely the same experience (were that even possible!); nor does it mean that we will comfort others by that most patronizing of phrases: 'I know how you feel'. We can never enter fully into the pain of another person, whether or not we have experienced something similar in our own lives. The way an individual suffers is always unique to him, for it depends upon the cumulative effect of many different events in his life and upon the inner resources which he can bring to bear on this particular pain. But at the same time we are not so different in our experiences that no communication, no reverberation of feeling is possible. In the majestic words of John Donne, describing 'for whom the bell tolls':

> No man is an ilande, intire of itself; every man is a peece of the Continent, a part of the maine . . . any man's deathe diminishes me, because I am involved in Mankinde; and therefore never send to know for whom the bell tolls; It tolls for thee.[13]

The wounded healer heals, because he is able to convey, as much by his presence as by the words he uses, both an awareness and a transcendence of loss. Of all human experiences, the experience of loss is the most pervasive and potentially the most crippling. It assails us from our earliest moments onward, when the security of womb, breast and infancy's small world are progressively replaced by the noise and frightening confusion of the outside world. Loss looms threateningly in the adult's life from the struggles of adolescents to find a secure independence to the fears of the ageing as disability and death approach.[14] Every person has many experiences of loss in his life, though frequently the defences erected against its pain have concealed almost totally the original source of hurt. The crippling effects are often felt only when a severe blow falls – a disabling illness, the loss of employment, a broken marriage, a bereavement. At other times unhealed loss may work on a person insidiously, the creeping paralysis of non-specific depression undermining hope and creativity.[15] The wounded healer heals because he, to some degree at least, has entered the depths of his own experiences of loss and in those depths has found hope again. The wounded healer has learned that it is useless to base his security on material possessions, on popularity and worldly success, even on the closest and most important of his personal relationships. He has learned (a little at least) from the Son of Man, who had nowhere to lay his head (Luke 9:58), and has understood the wisdom of Job's words: 'Naked I came from my mother's womb, naked I shall return' (Job 1:21 JB).

Thus the wounded healer helps others by his steadfast refusal to collude in their wish to avoid the reality of loss and the terror this can bring. As Henri Nouwen points out in his book *The Wounded Healer*, pastoral care does *not* remove pain: it deepens it.

> A minister is not a doctor whose primary task is to take away pain. Rather he deepens the pain to a level where it can be shared. . . .
>
> . . . Many people suffer because of the false supposition on which they have based their lives. That supposition is that there should be no fear or loneliness, no confusion or doubt. But these sufferings can only be dealt with creatively when they are understood as wounds integral to our human condition. Therefore ministry is a very confronting service. It does not allow people to live with illusions of immortality and wholeness. It keeps reminding others that they are mortal and broken, but also that with the recognition of this condition, liberation starts.[16]

It is at this elementary level of the refusal to offer palliative solutions that our care of others most frequently fails. It is not easy to oppose the illusions with which people try to soothe their unhappiness. (The difficulties are increased by the religious context of pastoral care, since a naive form of religious faith is frequently used as a defence against the harsh realities of life.[17] This means that to help others we often have to oppose such 'religion' in the name of faith.) When someone is desperately asking us to help them deny the reality of their pain, it requires strength to stay silent. Yet silence is often our greatest service. By remaining *with* people, but at the same time refusing to take the escape from pain they seek, we can restore their courage to voice their deepest fears and express the anguish they find so threatening. Our main task is to wait and watch with them, that simple service which Jesus asked for (in vain) from his friends.

In *The Christian Shepherd* Seward Hiltner quotes an interview with a recently bereaved woman which is an object lesson in how *not* to help another face grief. The minister visits the widow's home three weeks after the funeral, and (as Hiltner remarks) acts like 'a pastoral bulldozer':

PASTOR BARTON: So now his life with you is ended, and you cannot add to nor take away from it. Thus I want to tell you that all your thoughts about him must be self-analysed the moment they begin to cause you what is commonly called 'grief'. . . . Then if you find elements of self-pity, terminate them at once and force yourself to breathe a prayer of gratitude that your life with him was so beautiful and that he lived so complete a life in so short a time.[18]

'Pastor Barton' bullies the bereaved wife out of the mourning for her husband, which she must experience in order to learn to live without him. By encouraging her to deny her grief and to idealize the dead man, he is trying to cover over a wound which needs to be exposed to the air if it is to be healed.

A very different atmosphere is created in the following honest exchange between a bereaved farmer and his minister:

HARRY: . . . As kind as you were at the funeral, nothing that you said removed my grief. I even felt bitter when you read those words from the Bible about Jesus sending me another comforter. That's about the only words I remember from the service. I remember thinking to myself that

44

nothing could ever comfort me. I was pretty sceptical, believe me.

PASTOR: You no longer feel that way.

HARRY: That's the strange part of it, Reverend. Here I am, living as usual, making plans for the coming year, sowing my oats as I've done before. She isn't here with me, but yet I can feel her presence all around me. . . . Do you suppose that's the way God brings us comfort?[19]

The minister in this second interview is able to accept the 'scepticism' of the grieving husband. He does not try to 'play God', but acts as a quiet and reassuring witness to the man's *own* discovery that God brings healing in the depths of his despair.

What is the secret of such healing? How can hope come out of despair, comfort out of grief? It is not easy to answer this question, for the overcoming of suffering has a mysterious and transcendent quality to it, like the burst of life in spring after the cold emptiness of winter:

> Fields of our hearts that dead and bare have been:
> Love is come again,
> Like wheat that springeth green.[20]

We struggle with language which conveys the death and rebirth of the seed of life (1 Cor. 15:35–50), the dawning of light in deep darkness (Mat. 4:16), the restoration to wholeness of a body which seems utterly broken (Phil. 3:21). Perhaps the symbolism of the body offers the deepest insight, because it reminds us that the body of Christ, the Wounded Healer, lives on as the community of those who try to follow him (Rom. 12:5; Col. 1:18). It is evident that from the very beginning this body has been disjointed, torn apart by internal strife, disloyal to the cause of humble love to which it was called. Often the Christian churches put on the appearance of power and success, denying, with their show of comfort and self-confidence, the bleeding and despised body of their Lord. But new life can come to suffering people only when they find themselves in the company of those who, like Paul, are not ashamed to bear 'the marks of Jesus branded on (their) body' (Gal. 6:17 NEB). Healing comes within a community of sufferers, because there, where weakness is freely acknowledged, the power of God's love can enter in.[21] When there is the pretence of invulnerability and the denial of the raw and painful realities of life, the churches are drained of compassion and can tolerate only those who conceal their ill-health. To learn to care again, they need to hear the wisdom of T. S. Eliot's words:

> The wounded surgeon plies the steel
> That questions the distempered part;
> Beneath the bleeding hands we feel
> The sharp compassion of the healer's art.
> Resolving the enigma of the fever chart.
>
> Our only health is the disease
> If we obey the dying nurse
> Whose constant care is not to please
> But to remind of our, and Adam's curse,
> And that, to be restored, our sickness must grow worse.

* * * * *

> The dripping blood our only drink
> The bloody flesh our only food:
> In spite of which we like to think
> That we are sound, substantial flesh and blood –
> Again, in spite of that, we call this Friday good.[22]

5

Wise Folly

All things counter, original, spare, strange;
  Whatever is fickle, freckled (who knows how?)
  With swift, slow; sweet, sour; adazzle, dim;
He fathers-forth whose beauty is past change:
  Praise him.

Gerard Manley Hopkins, *Pied Beauty*[1]

The paradoxical insight that we heal most effectively by sharing our vulnerability leads to a third image by which pastoral care can be rediscovered: the dishevelled, gauche, tragi-comic figure of the fool. Paul's advice to the Corinthian church effectively dismisses worldly wisdom as a guideline for Christians:

If anyone among you thinks he is wise by this world's standards, he should become a fool, in order to be really wise.

(1 Cor. 3:18 TEV)

The fool is especially vulnerable to those who hold earthly power: easily derided and exploited, used as a scapegoat, treated (as Paul says in describing his own 'folly for Christ's sake') as 'the offal of the world . . . the scum of the earth' (1 Cor. 4:13 JB). Yet in all societies and all ages the fool has been a necessary and significant figure.[2] He appears as the essential counterpoise to human arrogance, pomposity and despotism. His unruly behaviour questions the limits of order; his 'crazy', outspoken talk probes the meaning of 'common sense'; his unconventional appearance exposes the pride and vanity of those around him; his foolhardy loyalty to 'lost' causes undercuts prudence and self-interest.

The more we examine it, the more complex and ambiguous

the image of the fool becomes. Folly is often two-edged, making mockery of good and ill alike, provoking malicious and cruel laughter at times, yet also using humour and ridicule to evoke love and concern. Since folly steps outside order, we cannot expect to control it easily – more often it takes us over in a holy or unholy madness. In this chapter I shall try to impose some order on the fool's image in order to see its significance for pastoral care, suggesting three dimensions of such care: folly as simplicity, folly as loyalty and folly as prophecy . . . but the feeling must remain that somewhere in the wings the fool is having the last laugh!

FOLLY AS SIMPLICITY

Søren Kierkegaard, reflecting in his journals upon the significance of the incarnation of Christ remarked: ' . . . one is sickened by the chatter of fussy go-betweens about Christ being the greatest hero, etc., etc., the humorous interpretation is far better.'[3] Kierkegaard had in mind the central paradox of Christianity that 'the eternal is the historical'.[4] He realized that to the logically minded such an idea must be plainly absurd, laughable, a cosmic joke. So it was that when Paul debated with the Epicurean and Stoic philosophers in Athens, some of them said contemptuously, 'Does this parrot know what he is talking about?' (Acts 17:18 JB). Similarly, Festus, the Roman Governor of Caesarea shouts out to Paul, when he declares that the Messiah had to suffer and then rise from the dead, 'Paul, you are raving; too much study is driving you mad' (Acts 26:24 NEB). Such reactions illustrate well Paul's own description of the effect his preaching had: ' . . . we proclaim the crucified Christ, a message that is offensive to the Jews and nonsense to the Gentiles' (1 Cor. 1:23 TEV).

How do we know when folly is a kind of wisdom and when it is simply nonsense? This is the first question which the ambiguous figure of the fool poses. In *The Exploits of the Incomparable Mulla Nasrudin*, Idries Shah has popularized an ancient figure of wise folly who originates in the mystical and intuitive insights of the Sufis of Islam. The Mulla is a highly entertaining character whose 'foolishness' often works to his advantage:

Time and again Nasrudin passed from Persia to Greece on

48

donkey-back. Each time he had two panniers of straw, and trudged back without them. Every time the guards searched him for contraband. They never found any.

'What are you carrying, Nasrudin?'

'I am a smuggler.'

Years later, more and more prosperous in appearance, Nasrudin moved to Egypt. One of the customs men met him there.

'Tell me, Mulla, now that you are out of the jurisdiction of Greece and Persia, living here in such luxury – what was it you were smuggling when we could never catch you?'

'Donkeys.'[5]

The wisdom of Mulla Nasrudin derives from the clever way in which his folly reveals the unexpected, the overlooked. The description of Touchstone in *As You Like It* fits the Mulla well: 'He uses his folly like a stalking horse and under the presentation of that he shoots his wit.'[6]

Such folly is undoubtedly a kind of wisdom and (as we shall see in a later section) the odd and surprising behaviour of the fool can provide a form of prophetic insight. But the folly of Christianity is less cunning, less contrived than the type of witty perception which is the stock in trade of the professional fool. Perhaps Erasmus is nearer the mark when he argues in his famous work *Praise of Folly*[7] that Christianity is close to a kind of natural simplicity. (We note that his remarks would now be viewed as deplorably sexist and 'age-ist'):

. . . the very young and the very old, women and simpletons are the people who take the greatest delight in sacred and holy things, and are therefore always found nearest the altars, led there doubtless solely by their natural instinct.[8]

Erasmus' reference to the simpleton or *'natural* fool' (a term used from medieval times to draw a contrast with the 'artificial fool', i.e. the professional court jester) heightens the ambiguity of the gospel's folly. For the natural fool lacks the *capacity* to reason. He speaks out of an intellectual innocence, unaware of the complexity of rational discourse. An obvious comparison may be drawn with Jesus' exhortation to his disciples to receive the Kingdom of God like little children (Luke 18:17), and with the simplicity of Jesus' own teaching, which depended not on complicated arguments but on vivid stories and dramatic actions. Thus Erasmus is prepared to describe Jesus himself as 'something of a fool':

> Christ, too, though he is the wisdom of the Father, was made something of a fool himself in order to help the folly of mankind, when he assumed the nature of man and was seen in man's form.[9]

Now we are indeed closer to the 'folly of the cross', for how are we to distinguish the naivety and intellectual incompetence of little children or of the mentally retarded from nonsense? Can we really say that such untutored simplicity is a form of wisdom? The question cannot be answered unambiguously. The 'natural fool' *does* lack knowledge and reasoning ability. He frequently fails to understand the more complex aspects of human experience, and his lack of ability to predict consequences can at times endanger himself and others. Yet this same lack of sophistication gives a refreshing directness to the simpler person's ways of relating to others. There is a physical immediacy in his responses of affection and anger and a lack of hypocrisy in the things he says. (One can understand how the 'natural fool' was the precursor of the professional court fool, who had a licence to speak hard truths to the King.)[10]

Dostoyevsky's novel, *The Idiot*, provides an interesting portrayal of the effect which an (apparently) simple-minded person can have on those around him. The principal character Prince Myshkin (who is an epileptic, as Dostoyevsky himself was) appears slow-witted and socially gauche. His open simplicity of manner leads people to regard him as an idiot, especially since he does not conform to the insincerities and cynical self-seeking of the upper-class society to which he belongs. His honesty and simplicity expose the corruptions of the people around him, yet in a gentle and perceptive manner which seems to offer them a way back to their true selves. The effect he creates on people is well summed up by Ganya, a character who is at once fascinated by Prince Myshkin and furious at his simple honesty:

> ' . . . what made me think this morning that you were an idiot? You notice things other people never notice. One

could have a real talk to you, though, perhaps, one had better not.'[11]

The wisdom of such simplicity lies in its power to expose insincerity and self-deception. Often the simple person is unaware of the effect he is having on those around him, and (unlike the professional fool) he is not acting the way he does *in order* to create an effect. Yet he mediates singleness and honesty to those who have ears to hear him and eyes to see him. It is as though he holds up a mirror in which we can see a reflection of our society's and our own hypocrisy.[12]

Those of us who are adult and in full possession of our faculties cannot, of course, pretend to possess the simplicity of the natural fool. We cannot make ourselves into innocent little children or dispossess ourselves of our reasoning powers. Indeed, it would be a strange denial of ourselves to want to do so. But the image of folly as simplicity can help us rediscover parts of ourselves which have been lost, as we learned 'adult wisdom', thus opening up more spontaneous ways of relating to ourselves and others. That same simplicity can remind us that faith is a product of trust not of reason and that such trust comes more easily to those who do not insist on intellectualizing every experience. Rediscovering simplicity can also make us less afraid of speaking nonsense in the world's estimation, for such 'nonsense' can often strike at the heart of truth.

How these aspects of the simplicity of folly may improve our pastoral care will be discussed at the end of the chapter, after we have examined two other dimensions of folly, loyalty and prophecy.

FOLLY AS LOYALTY

A second dimension of folly brings us to the notion of *foolhardiness*. The folly of the cross, and therefore of those who try to obey Jesus' call to take up *their* cross and follow him, is the sheer lack of self-interest which such action entails. As Paul continues to pursue the theme of folly in his first letter to the Corinthians, he is moved to draw some invidious comparisons between his converts' life and his own:

. . . it seems to me that God has given the very last place

51

to us apostles. . . . For Christ's sake we are fools; but you are wise in union with Christ! We are weak, but you are strong! We are despised, but you are honoured! To this very moment we go hungry and thirsty; we are clothed in rags; we are beaten; we wander from place to place; we wear ourselves out with hard work. . . . We are no more than this world's refuse. . . .

(1 Cor. 4: 9–13 TEV)

Paul had a tendency to get carried away with self-admiration when describing the rigours of his life (as he himself was aware (2 Cor. 11:17)); but the purpose of this 'boasting' was to remind his fellow-Christians that loyalty to Christ must mean hardship and the risking of self: 'I am content with weaknesses, insults, hardships, persecutions, and difficulties for Christ's sake. For when I am weak, then I am strong' (2 Cor. 12:10 TEV). The loyalty of the fool who follows Christ is an enigma in the world's eyes – the greater the loyalty, the greater the suffering which ensues. Why then remain loyal, if there is no advantage to it?

The same enigma is presented in dramatic form by the character of the Fool in Shakespeare's *King Lear*. The play depicts the sharp contrast between the misunderstood loyalty of Cordelia, Kent and the Fool and the falsely trusted flattery of Goneril, Regan and Edmund. The King discovers too late who his real enemies are, and, as his madness mounts, the fury of a stormy night matches his inner turmoil. Now, cast out into the storm by his heartless daughters, the half-crazed old man finds that his only companion is the Fool who 'labours to outjest his heart-struck injuries'.[13] Why does the Fool stay by the King's side when everyone else deserts him? In typical style, the Fool explains himself in a little ditty:

> That sir which serves and seeks for gain,
>> And follows but for form,
> Will pack when it begins to rain
>> And leave thee in the storm.
> But I will tarry; the fool will stay,
>> And let the wise man fly:
> The knave turns fool that runs away;
>> The fool no knave perdy.[14]

Against the greed, treachery and callous disregard for others which now dominates Lear's former kingdom, the Fool presents the simple virtue of an unheroic, but persistent loyalty. Shame lies not in being a fool, but in being a knave.[15]

This enigma – the strange willingness to disregard self out of a higher loyalty – can be found at the centre of Jesus' life and death. The taunting of the dying Jesus by the chief priests, scribes and elders focuses on the helpless state of the one who, it was claimed, was King of Israel and Son of God: 'He saved others; himself he cannot save. . . . He trusted in God; let him deliver him now' (Mat. 27:42f AV). The mockery echoes the temptations in the wilderness when Jesus refused to seek power and safety by supernatural means (Luke 4:1–13 and par.). Instead, he chose the foolhardy way, the unprotected path that led to danger and death.

Such foolhardiness is also a prominent feature of Jesus' teaching. Some of his sayings and stories draw attention to the *wrong* kind of foolishness: There is the fool who builds a house on sand instead of on rock (Mat. 7:24–27 and par.); the fool who enlarges his barns and neglects his soul (Luke 12:13–21); and the five female fools who are caught unprepared for the coming of the bridegroom (Mat. 25:1–13). Yet at the same time Jesus encourages a quite outrageous improvidence in his followers: they must deny themselves to follow him (Mat. 16:24); a man cannot stay to bury his father or turn back to say goodbye to his family (Luke 9: 59–62); the rich young man must sell all he has (Mat. 19:16–22); family and possessions are rightly left behind for the Kingdom's sake (Mark 10:29 and par.); and no thought is to be taken for the morrow:

> And so I tell you not to worry about the food you need to stay alive or about the clothes you need for your body. Life is much more important than food, and the body much more important than clothes.
>
> (Luke 12:22f TEV)

The force of all this teaching may be summed up in the mysterious saying of Jesus: 'Whosoever will save his life shall lose it: and whosoever will lose his life for my sake will find it' (Mat. 16:25 AV). It is useless to try to take away the sharpness of this saying by the glib explanation that since faith brings a higher fulfilment, there is really no danger of loss for the Christian. Such an easy solution translates follow-

53

ing Jesus into enlightened self-interest, and thereby removes the folly of the cross. The whole point of the fool's loyalty is that he *cannot* be sure it will be to his advantage. His loyalty is the very opposite of prudence, because, on the face of it, he is risking comfort and life itself for some unattainable ideal. He would be no fool at all if he already knew that everything would turn out all right. (One of the lessons the first Christians had to learn was that their hopes for an early coming of the Kingdom of God, when love and justice would finally prevail, were mistaken. No such easy reassurance presented itself.)

All the fool for Christ's sake can know is that to be true to himself he must try to be loyal to Christ and that this must mean putting love and service to others first in his life. The enigma of such loyalty finds its ultimate expression in the crazy logic of loving those who do you harm:

> Love your enemies, do good to those who hate you, bless those who curse you, and pray for those who ill-treat you.
> (Luke 6:27f TEV)

Jesus surely appears to be the greatest of fools when he asks God to forgive his accusers and executioners even as they mock him in his suffering. How could a person allow himself to be so exploited, unless he trusted beyond reason, in the ultimate triumph of love? As we shall see, the same question faces those who try to be the givers of care in much less extreme situations of mockery and hurt. There is nothing more easily exploited than the loyalty of the fool.[16]

FOLLY AS PROPHECY

So far we have been examining what may be called the 'pathetic' aspects of the fool's image, the fool as a simpleton, and the fool as a loyal, easily exploited friend. But there is also a more active, rumbustious, resilient aspect to the fool, which must not be neglected. This comic aspect gives a quite different perspective to the nature of folly. It reveals it to be a form of *prophecy*, not in the sense of *fore*telling the future, but in the sense of *forth*telling, of pointing to the signs of the times and proclaiming divine revelations about them.[17] The prophetic aspect of folly has, throughout the ages, functioned as a form

of challenge to the accepted norms, conventions and authorities within a society. Thus Wolfgang Zucker can argue that
the modern circus clown is a vehicle of God's laughter at
man's arrogance and self-importance:

> Who laughs? Is it the clown, the marginal outsider; or is
> it the audience when it is taken to and beyond the limits
> of its own restricting order? Or still another possibility: is
> not the clown perhaps himself the laughter of the Infinite
> about the Finite when it pretends to be absolute? The
> laughter of God?[18]

An interesting historical example of the use of folly as a
challenge to ecclesiastical authority is found in the medieval
Narrenfest, the Feast of Fools. This was a kind of anti-Mass
celebrated by the younger clergy in defiance of the bishop
and his established orders. Beginning on the first of January
(the Day of Circumcision) it continued until Epiphany. The
'celebrants' wore masks and fantastic costumes, banqueted at
the altar, celebrated an obscene parody of the ritual of the
Mass and even, on occasion, worshipped an ass as the 'Lord
of Disorder'. Despite official opposition the practice was followed in many European cathedral churches from the twelfth
to the fifteenth century and vestiges of it can be found as late
as the seventeenth century.[19] Such frolics can be regarded as
a kind of safety valve, allowing the expression of forbidden
wishes which the usual pomp and solemnity of religious ritual
cannot allow, but they also have a deeper significance. They
raise questions about the undue importance with which religious institutions invest themselves. Thus such dramatic foolery is moving in the direction of the Old Testament prophets'
challenge to the practice of cultic sacrifices:

> What shall I bring when I approach the Lord?
>   How shall I stoop before God on high?
> Am I to approach him with whole-offerings or yearling
> calves?
>   Will the Lord accept thousands of rams
>   or ten thousand rivers of oil?
> Shall I offer my eldest son for my wrongdoing,
>   my children for my own sin?

The dramatic exaggeration of Micah's descriptions, culmi-
nating in the horror of human sacrifice, creates a parody of

priestly worship and prepares the hearer for the contrast of the prophet's own message:

> God has told you what is good;
>> and what is it that the Lord asks of you?
> Only to act justly, to love loyalty,
> to walk wisely before your God.

(Micah 6: 6–8 NEB)

The creation of such dramatic effects is still more evident in the bizarre *behaviour* of the Old Testament prophets. By means of symbolic actions,[20] reminiscent of the 'crazy' antics of the professional clown, they drew attention to God's judgement on Israel. For example, Isaiah went naked[21] and barefoot for three years to warn of the impending humiliation and captivity of Egypt and Cush (Isa. 20:1–6); Hosea married a prostitute[22] and gave ominous names to her children (Hos. 1:2–9). Jeremiah hid a waist-cloth in a crevice among rocks (Jer. 13:1–11); walked around with a yoke on his back (Jer. 27:1–11); and threw a book containing prophecies of disaster into the Euphrates, weighting it with a stone (Jer. 51:59–64). Ezekiel cut off his hair and beard, burned some in the centre of the city, cut some up and scattered the rest to the wind (Ezek. 5:1–14); he packed his belongings and left the city like an exile (Ezek. 12:1–11); and he failed to show signs of mourning when his wife died (Ezek. 24:15–24). When we add to these strange actions of the prophets their ecstatic utterances and dramatic visions, it is no surprise to read that Hosea was accused of being a crazy fool (Hos. 9:7) or that Jeremiah was in danger of being locked up as a madman (Jer. 29:26f).

Such strange behaviour, however, is madness only to those who are too set in their ways to hear the prophet's message. The whole point of prophecy is that it does not fit in with the 'common-sense' assumptions of the day: it cuts cross-grained to earthly power and authority, announcing God's judgement upon it. Thus it is often misunderstood, ridiculed or simply ignored. There is something elusive about such incongruity. You need to have ears to hear it and eyes to see it:

> He stays quite motionless, while
> all else functions as it should;
> dead-in-the-centre, odd, futile,
>
> no use for anything, no good;

symbolises contradiction,
that which can't be understood,

incongruity, restriction
disparity and ridicule;
fact that out-imagines fiction,

exception made to prove the rule.
Who can close his eyes to see
the lightning movements of the Fool?[23]

The same element of incongruity may be seen in the prophetic words and actions of Jesus. He reverses the accepted religious values of his day, making the humble tax-gatherer more righteous than the law-abiding Pharisee (Luke 18: 10–14), the Samaritan more loving than the priest and the Levite (Luke 10:25–37), the rich man less acceptable than the poor (Luke 18:25 and par.). He associates with the 'wrong' company (Luke 15:1f) and fails to fast and abstain from wine like other prophets (Luke 7:34). He defies the legalism of the Sabbath laws by allowing his disciples to pluck ears of corn and by healing a man with a paralysed hand (Luke 6:1–11 and par.).[24]

The drama of Jesus' prophetic actions and the colourful and paradoxical imagery of his teachings have been captured in an attractive way in the musical, *Godspell*, which portrays Jesus and his followers as a troupe of playful and irreverent clowns. *Godspell* succeeds in restoring the humour and gaiety in the life of Jesus, which (in view of the criticisms made by the religious authorities of his time) must have been present, but was quickly lost in the solemnity of pious memories.[25] The guise of the clown also conveys some of the pathos of the gospel narrative, for the clown's appearance is at once both comic and tragic. But the clown's costume is also an inadequate portrayal of the depth of folly in the passion of Jesus. Here Jesus' words about the strange appearance of John the Baptist apply:

'What was the spectacle that drew you to the wilderness? A reed-bed swept by the wind? No? Then what did you go out to see? A man dressed in silks and satins?'

(Luke 7:24f NEB)

The appearance which Jesus presents as his death approaches vividly conveys the reversal of values which his whole life represented: 'He had no beauty, no majesty to draw our eyes' (Isa. 53:2 NEB). Before his betrayal and arrest, he stripped off his clothing and wearing only a cloth round his waist, like the humblest slave, he washed the feet of his disciples (John 13:3ff). Then before he is led out to be crucified, the Roman soldiers strip off his clothes once more, and, in mockery of his kingship, dress him in a purple robe and a crown of thorny branches. The 'kingly' costume forced on to Jesus makes mockery of his accusers, not of him, since his kingship was not of this world and the humility of a condemned prisoner was his royal choice. Jesus, incongruously clad as slave and as mock king, challenges all who arrogate to themselves a place of special importance in this world or the next.

Thus folly can function as a potent form of prophecy, because, by its startling reversal of the shaft of ridicule, it allows us to see ourselves in a clearer light and prevents us from giving to fallible human institutions the honour they are *not* due. Yet we must beware of supposing that *all* folly is prophetic in this way. Clowning, buffoonery and satire can often be heartless, destructive of human values, a weapon to protect the perpetrator against any genuine involvement with others.[26] Frequently, the professional fool functions merely as a mouthpiece for the hidden desires of his audience, allowing them to identify with his excess of vulgarity and violence without feeling a sense of responsibility for it themselves. Again, much professional foolery finds its origins in a cruel mockery of 'freaks', that is the mentally subnormal, physically deformed or emotionally damaged members of society. In fact, the human capacity for laughter and for delight in the unusual can be used in an amazing variety of ways, for good or ill. But the capacity to laugh also points to an essentially human attribute, the ability to reflect upon experience.[27] It is this self-reflective ability which makes *homo ridens* into a creature who can respond to the challenge of prophecy, and, in turn, allows us to regard prophetic folly as an aspect of pastoral care.

PASTORAL CARE AS FOLLY

In *Pastoral Care in the Modern Hospital*, Heije Faber suggests that we can compare the minister working in a hospital with the clown in the circus. The clown's role, according to Faber, contains three tensions: he is one of many circus acts, yet he has a certain uniqueness, setting him apart from the others; he appears and feels like an amateur amongst highly skilled professionals; and his act is one of creative spontaneity, yet it demands study and training. Faber implies that the clown to be truly a clown must never seem quite at home in the circus, and he has little difficulty in showing that a minister in the modern hospital is (or should be) in the same position. What the minister has to offer is different in kind from the many professional skills encompassed by the health care professions.[28]

The analogy drawn by Faber can be broadened out to apply to pastoral care as a whole, not simply to the pastoral work of ministers working in hospital settings. Just as the clown act is unique in the circus, so pastoral care must be *in* the world, but not *of* the world. It must operate within modern society, recognizing its powerful effects on people, but it can never fit comfortably into it. A caring which is pastoral must always seem a little bizarre, a little naive, and not a little irreverent, in the context of the values which our materialistic culture worships. Moreover, pastoral care must avoid the temptation to turn its 'clown act' into the polished perform-ance of the trapeze artiste, the lion tamer, or the juggler. The folly, the scandal of pastoral care is that it describes the stumbling efforts of the non-professional to care for others. Some words about the sense of identification which the circus clown evokes in his audience might equally be applied to the attractiveness and fallibility of ordinary human caring:

> In him, in his ludicrous contradictions of dignity and em-barrassment, of pomp and rags, of assurance and collapse, of sentiment and sadness, of innocence and guile, we learn to see ourselves.[29]

Thus the tendency in recent pastoral care literature to focus almost exclusively on 'counselling skills' and to encourage the development of a cadre of professional 'pastoral counsellors' must be viewed with some alarm. Such developments create a 'competence gap' between professional, trained counsellors and the 'ordinary' church member and easily result in a loss of the uniquely *foolish* aspects of pastoral care.[30] On the other hand, the foolish aspects of caring are not to be equated with the blundering (if well-meant) incompetence of the person who has not troubled to prepare himself for the task of helping others. As Faber reminds us, the clown's refreshing spontaneity is the product of careful preparation and training. The same must be true of the folly of our pastoral care. It will be helpful to others only when we learn how to acquire the simplicity, loyal love and releasing laughter of God's 'foolishness'. Such qualities rarely come naturally to us. They need some kind of learning.

Simplicity

Let us then return to the simplicity of the fool and consider how we might try to identify with it. The greatest hazard facing us in trying to help others is our verbosity. We use words to distance ourselves from experience – our own and other people's – and so to lose the simple sense of *nearness* – nearness of nature, of other people and of God. The loss of this unitary vision permits us to be seduced into playing verbal games with people instead of seeking with them that which brings them peace. In Kahlil Gibran's words: '. . . thought is a bird of space, that in a cage of words may indeed unfold its wings, but cannot fly.'[31] To rediscover the simplicity of the natural fool we need to find ways of release from the 'cage of words'. Thus preparation for caring means learning to enjoy the richness of silence, not as a hard ascetic discipline, but as a refreshment and a delight. From this grounding in silence we can learn to respond in simpler ways to our own bodies, learning to be more at home in them and to rejoice in the richness of sense-experience which is continually offered to us through them. This in turn can open up our vision of the outer world, preventing us from constantly snatching from it only that which will serve our immediate purposes, restoring a childlike vision:

> To see a World in a Grain of Sand
> And a heaven in a Wild Flower
> Hold Infinity in the palm of your hand
> And Eternity in an hour.[32]

Music offers another avenue to simplicity, since it communicates both spontaneity and order at a level which words cannot reach. In responding to its mysterious powers of rhythm, sound and silence, we are released from the domination of clock time, with its measured reminders of passing minutes and hours, and are free to enter the world of the simple fool, where all is immediacy and where anxiety has no sway over us. We no longer need to justify each moment by what has been achieved in it, but can appreciate time, not as demand, but as gift.

If we are willing to prepare ourselves in these foolish ways, we can bring rich resources of help to others. The person who knows silence and immediacy as friends will no longer feel worried about knowing the right *words* to say to others. He will not need to justify himself in his own eyes by being a 'successful' and admired helper of the needy. His help will emanate from a simple enjoyment of getting close to a fellow human being who welcomes his company. (To the little man perched up a tree, Jesus says, 'Hurry down, Zacchaeus, because I must stay in your house to-day.' (Luke 19:5 TEV) How could a busy man like Jesus spare such time?) The simple fool brings no baggage with him when another seeks his help, no techniques, no 'pastoral medicine bag'. When pretence is stripped aside, all we fools have to offer one another is 'a condition of complete simplicity, costing not less than everything'.[33] Few of us manage to be so foolish.

Loyal Love

But now a great worry which must face us when we consider so simplified an approach to pastoral care: the fear of loss of control. When care is offered by a professional agency, in the form of social casework, medical care, educational assistance, legal advice, etc., there are numerous devices for protecting the professional helper (and to a lesser extent, his client) against exploitation. Access to help is controlled by appointment systems, by cost limitations and by referrals to other agencies; the liability of the helper is limited to the area of professional competence to which he lays claim; and the personal life of the helper is strictly segregated from his professional life. These devices protect both professional and client against the hazards of over-involvement. Thus, even in the intense encounters of professional psychotherapy, the helping relationship remains strictly a business one, offered within stated hours and according to a defined set of rules.

The folly of pastoral care, at least as I have been describing it, is that it refuses to operate within these protective limitations. It foolishly offers love. It is therefore a foolhardy activity which may result in the exploitation of both helper and helped. This danger is seen most clearly in the tendency for helping relationships to foster a destructive form of dependency. Such dependency is always mutual: not only does the person seeking help make childish and unrealistic demands on the time and attention of the helper; the helper (consciously or unconsciously) encourages such dependency, acquiescing in and even encouraging each unreasonable demand. Helper and helped alike are caught within a ring of fear, each one as frightened as the other of being left alone and unloved. (Of course, the helper rationalizes his over-attentiveness by saying that it is the other's need to which he responds, failing to see the forces of anxiety which prevent him from saying No to the other's demands.) In view of such dangers it is important to distinguish the loyalty of the fool from such mutual evasions of responsibility, masquerading under the name of care. The fool is vulnerable precisely because of his refusal to take part in such self-protective manoeuvres. 'Prithee nuncle', says Lear's Fool, 'keep a schoolmaster that can teach thy fool to lie: I would fain learn to lie.'[34] The fool can be hurt and exploited because he must speak the truth even if this inevitably brings anger on his own head. There is nothing collusive about the loving loyalty of the fool: not for him the easy comfort of the appeaser and flatterer. The fool for Christ's sake trusts in love and that must mean the love that lets go, not the over-protectiveness which denies reality and coddles the other person.

Perhaps this is the hardest lesson to learn in the art of caring, because it means setting our own limits on relationships, without the aid of receptionists, office-hours or professional codes of practice. We often confuse over-involvement in others' troubles with Christian love and fail to risk the unpopularity of refusing to meet others' expectations of us. Yet Jesus resisted the insatiable demands of the crowds in order to pray in solitude (Luke 9:18); and his love for his disciples meant leaving them without a leader (but not without the comfort of his Spirit) to face persecution and ridicule.[35] For us, loving loyalty will often mean staying close to others, when they need us and when others have turned their backs on them; but equally loving loyalty can mean trusting in God's all-pervading love, when we see that the best way to help another is to enable him to reject us and let go of us. Then we seem poor fools indeed, since our loving heaps coals of fire on *our* heads.

Laughter in Heaven
Yet how serious the folly of pastoral care is now becoming, it seems! Fortunately for us and for those we try to help, our folly need not always be such a solemn matter. (It would be, no doubt, if we really believed that the cure of all the world's woes depended on the success of our erratic efforts to care.) It seems more realistic to suggest that our folly can at best save people from putting their trust in false idols, helping them to question any grandiose claims for the betterment of mankind.

In a discussion of Paul Tillich's use of terms like 'depth of being' and 'ultimate concern', Alan Watts wonders whether joy in the presence of God has got to be such an awesome experience:

> Does anyone really want the End, the Final Ground of all things, to be *completely* serious? No twinkle? No gaiety? Something rigid and overwhelming and ponderously real? Such a profound seriousness might be the ante-room, but not the presence chamber.[36]

If instead there is laughter in heaven, as Watts suggests[37], then a major part of our witness to love is to encourage laughter on earth. In saying this, I am not seeking to invoke the image of the 'jolly parson', who spreads a false cheerfulness in a denial of pain. Rather, it is the carefree image of the fool which must reappear, as an expression of the joyousness of faith. Such a reappearance of laughter might help us to save the churches from their obsession with decency, order and respectability and allow them to offer a genuine alternative to the images of power and material prosperity which dominate 'developed' societies. Pastoral care needs to become prophetic, mediating a new and strangely different attitude to life, leaving people wondering whether to laugh *at* it or *with* it, tapping into the well of laughter of God's revelation of himself:

> His laughter lifting from despair,
> welling up within mankind

as if in truth he's always there;
to level us perhaps, and save us
from ourselves — if we could dare —

The Fool, the God, the one who gave us
himself, expressed in one man's face,
the sense of his humour, and called it grace.[38]

Thus churches which are capable of laughing at themselves, of admitting their fallibility and frequent descents into the ridiculous, will be better able to speak with a prophetic voice to the alienating and dehumanizing powers of our age. And individuals who have a lightness of touch, an informality based on amusement at their own ineptitude, bring the simplest of gifts to others — the releasing power of laughter.

6

The Cavern

If the doors of perception were cleansed
every thing would appear to man as it is,
infinite.
For man has closed himself up, till he sees
all things through narrow chinks of his cavern.

William Blake, *The Marriage of Heaven and Hell*[1]

Up to this point I have been trying to view pastoral relationships from the perspective of the person offering care, seeking
images by which to understand the nature of that offer. In
this chapter and the next I shall be changing the direction of
vision, looking for insight into the needs which people are
expressing when they ask for, or accept, pastoral care. Since
I have already stressed the mutuality of pastoral relationships
(see Chapter One), I do not regard this as a radical change
of perspective. Much of what I have already said about the
lack of courage, vulnerability and folly of the helper is by
implication a description of the needs of the person who seeks
help. If we help out of weakness then we are no strangers to
it (Heb. 4:15); but now it is necessary to bring together the
various aspects of need which have been implied in my descriptions of pastoral care as loving leadership, wounded healing and wise folly. The traditional approach to all 'spiritual
ills' has been to regard them as originating in two sources:
sinfulness and lack of faith. Using these traditional descriptions as a starting point, I shall be suggesting that what
people are seeking from pastoral care is *liberation* from the
cavern of sin and *companionship* on the *journey of faith*.

Yet is it really possible to take 'sinfulness' as a starting point for understanding the needs of our present age? We seem to see in our contemporaries a loss of the sense of sin[2] and a tendency to dismiss all feelings of guilt as childish or neurotic. Much confusion about the nature of sin and guilt has arisen from the (erroneous) impression that psychotherapy – in particular Freudian psychoanalysis – has somehow undermined modern man's moral sensibility. Thus O. H. Mowrer can write:

> From the testimony now available from both friends and foes of psycho-analysis, it is clear that, at best, analysis casts a spell but does not cure. By aligning himself with the patient's id, the analyst ('Devil'?) may indeed succeed in suspending the superego; but the superego (or conscience), more commonly than we might wish to believe, is a reflection of enduring social realities; and the advantage we gain by overcoming it is dearly paid for later, many times over.[3]

Mowrer's attack on Freud betrays a woeful ignorance of the theory and methods of psychoanalysis, but since he represents a common misunderstanding it is important to examine briefly what Freud did in fact say about the nature of guilt. We shall discover that his work (and that of subsequent psychotherapeutic theorists) performs a useful 'ground clearing' exercise for a contemporary understanding of the pastoral dimensions of guilt.[4]

The Freudian Superego

It is essential to realize that the primary function of Freud's study of guilt was to explain the origin of the psychoneuroses and thereby to aid in the attempts of psychoanalysis to cure mental illness. Thus the phenomena of conscience which he describes are by definition destructive of the health of the individual and maladaptive for his life in society. According to Freud's theory, the superego or 'conscience' is formed as a result of the young child's encounter with parental discipline. As the forbidden wishes of his pleasure-seeking 'id' come in conflict with the commands and prohibitions issued by his parents a state of great anxiety is created. The child eventually attempts to resolve this by 'introjecting' the prohibiting voice of the parent – in other words, by acquiring a 'conscience'. At the same time the child may internalize *positive* aspects of his relationship with his parents, using them as models to emulate (the 'ego ideal'). But if the superego has been created largely out of anxiety and of fear of the loss of love, then the *negative* conscience outweighs the *positive* ego-ideal, leading to a personality conflict which endures to adult life and expresses itself in various types of neurosis. The cure for such neurosis must lie in releasing the adult from the power of this parental authority and giving his 'ego' (his conscious, rational self) a greater say in the planning, control and evaluation of his actions. ('Where superego was, there shall ego be.')[5]

In his later writings Freud added a starker, gloomier hue to this account of the negative conscience, a gloom deriving from his postulation of a 'death instinct' (*thanatos*), an innate destructiveness in man. This belief in a death instinct affected Freud's theory of conscience in two ways. Firstly it made the creation of a negative conscience the *sine qua non* of civilization. Since man was by nature utterly self-seeking, rapacious and murderous, he could live peacefully with others only through massive 'instinctual renunciation' which necessitated a powerfully repressive conscience (often bolstered by the threats and promises of religion). Secondly, the conscience itself was regarded as largely 'internalized aggression' (parental destructiveness incorporated in the child) and thus inevitably cruel, punishing and vindictive in character.

We are now able to see the relevance of the Freudian account of guilt to a modern approach to pastoral care. His theory reveals the danger of confusing *feelings of guilt* with an awareness of the sin which entraps us all. A person suffering from a depressive illness, for example, can experience a level of guilt quite out of proportion to any specific actions which might normally be regarded as wrong (by himself or by others). Moreover, the depressed person's guilt feelings have a never-ending quality to them. They do not lead to altered behaviour, nor do they diminish in response to arguments which point out their unreasonableness. (Father confessors of the past were familiar with this phenomenon, and called it 'scrupulosity.') Freud convincingly showed that such guilt feelings are related, not to external realities, but to internal ones. They are the product of conflict between different parts of a disintegrated personality.[6] Such disintegrative guilt feelings are not restricted to those who can be labelled 'mentally ill'. Each one of us has almost certainly experienced to some degree the 'superego' conflict which Freud describes, since we find it difficult to dissociate ourselves from the powerful influence of parental authority, even in our adult lives and even after our parents' death. It is most important not to give such feelings of childish guilt a greater moral significance than they in fact merit. They merely reflect the *dissonance* between our behaviour and our parents' beliefs about how we should act. They do not tell us whether we are *right* to feel guilty. That is a question of a quite different kind, whose answer bears no relationship to the severity of the guilt we may feel as a result of our ambivalent feelings towards our parents and their morality.

But what of the gloomier side of Freud's account of guilt? Is he right in supposing that a negative and vindictive conscience is the best we can hope for in this life especially if civilization is to be maintained? In considering this question, I shall summarize the views of a markedly optimistic, post-Freudian psychotherapist, Carl Rogers.

Rogers and the Doctrine of Acceptance

Rogers believes that man is unhappy, self-destructive and anti-social basically because he cannot accept himself as he really is. He locates the blame for this lack of self-acceptance on social conditioning. From the earliest stages of upbringing the child learns that parts of himself are unacceptable, dirty, shameful or bad. He therefore begins to see himself as a person only of *conditional* worth. He will be valued and loved by his parents and other important adults *only if* he denies some aspects of himself, pretending that they are not really part of him. Eventually these externally imposed values are introjected so that whole parts of the person's experience are excluded from his 'self concept'. The result is a sense of guilt whenever the unacceptable parts of himself attempt to gain expression.

The goal of Rogerian psychotherapy is to help the individual 'become that self he truly is'[7] by offering a relationship characterized by empathy, openness and acceptance. Of these three qualities, acceptance is the most potent in overcoming guilt, since it communicates 'a warm regard for (the client) as a person of unconditional self-worth – of value no matter what his condition, his behaviour, his feelings'.[8] As a result of this experience in psychotherapy the client will begin to free himself from externally imposed judgements and to find 'a locus of evalution' within himself. This change is described as moving *away* from façades, 'oughts', meeting expectations, pleasing others and *towards* self-direction, process, complexity, openness to experience, acceptance of others and trust of self. The client becomes 'a fully functioning person'.[9]

For Rogers, then, the only possible standard by which each person is to be judged is his awareness of *his own being* in all its complexity. The external standard is always seen as an intrusion, a falling away from the true morality of self-direction. Moreover, Rogers believes that *only* by encouraging individuals to be more self-accepting will we ensure that they act co-operatively with their fellow men. Freud claimed that without the introjected constraints of society's morality men would destroy each other. But Rogers believes that it is *precisely these constraints* which are to blame for man's destructive aggressiveness; remove them, shift the locus of evaluation to the individual himself, and it will turn out that his impulses are trustworthy and in harmony with the needs of others:

> When we are able to free the individual from defensiveness, so that he is open to the wide range of his own needs, as well as the wide range of environmental and social demands, his reactions may be trusted to be positive, forward-moving, constructive.
>
> I have little sympathy with the rather prevalent concept that man is basically irrational, and that his impulses, if not controlled, will lead to destruction of others and self.[10]

Thus according to Rogers acceptance leads to social harmony and to a self-chosen personal morality. From a theological point of view Rogers might be seen as providing a secularized version of the doctrine of grace: unconditional love frees us from the dead letter of the law and fills us with a new spirit.[11]

Once again we can see that insights gained from psychotherapy help to clear the ground for pastoral care. Rogers has fixed on the important point that a morality which is not truly one's own, but is merely external conformity to someone

69

else's value judgements, can bring only a self-destructive form of guilt. He correctly opposes and rejects a morality based on shame and hatred of self, and identifies the experience of acceptance as the source of respect for both oneself and others. Yet is his trust in the goodness of the self-directing individual really justified? As we compare the theories of Rogers and Freud on this point we realize that we are encountering two opposing sets of basic assumptions. Freud starts with the assumption that the individual is innately selfish and destructive and regards any apparent evidence of altruism as simply a covert form of selfishness or of masochistic self-denial. Rogers, on the other hand, has faith in the reasonableness and co-operativeness of each individual and attributes any evidence of selfishness to the destructive effects of an inhumane society. Each theorist finds the evidence he needs to 'prove' his case.

The theologian, concerned to relate the experience of guilt to a doctrine of sin, cannot rest content with either account of the human predicament. The Freudian view leaves us without hope, caught between the inexorable forces of Eros and Thanatos, the victims of a punishing and ultimately pointless guilt. But the Rogerian view is only apparently more liberating. It merely locks each person inside the prison of his own individuality, encouraging him to believe that openness, flexibility and self-acceptance will of themselves bring wisdom and fulfilment.[12] Rogers excludes the tragic dimension from human existence, failing to see that guilt (though at times inappropriate and untrue to the reality of the individual as a whole) can also reveal aspects of human failure which the individual cannot remedy on his own. In both Freud and Rogers the *transcendent* element in guilt is disregarded, that element which points beyond the fallible moral values of parents and society to the basic state of lostness and alienation we call sin. Nicolas Berdyaev has accurately pointed out the dangers to modern man entailed in his loss of such an awareness:

> At different times and in different ways man has been conscious of sin, of an ancient burden of guilt, of his participation in a fallen world. This was an expression of his deep feeling for life; and if modern man has lost the sense of sin and of the Fall, it is a sign that he has also lost his

70

spirituality and is leading a superficial existence at the mercy of the world.[13]

The Cavern
How then may the experience of guilt restore 'a deep feeling for life' and save us from 'a superficial existence at the mercy of the world'? Given that we have discarded (or at least attempted to discard) the false guilt of moralism, we may see two sources of a more profound experience of guilt: awareness of time and awareness of others. These two aspects of our awareness each carry a sad sense of *lost opportunity*, a feeling of being overwhelmed by the complexity of life. Two images, the cavern and the river, express this lostness.

Rabindranath Tagore reflects on the poverty of our awareness in a beautiful prose poem contemplating the approach of death:

> I know that the day will come when my sight of this earth shall be lost, and life will take its leave in silence, drawing the last curtain over my eyes.
>
> Yet stars will watch at night, and morning rise as before, and hours heave like sea waves casting up pleasures and pains.
>
> When I think of this end of my moments, the barrier of the moments breaks and I see by the light of death thy world with its careless treasures. Rare is its lowliest seat, rare is its meanest of lives.
>
> Things that I longed for in vain and things that I got – let them pass. Let me but truly possess the things that I ever spurned and overlooked.[14]

Tagore's words reveal the darkness in our lives, the cavern in which we dwell. We rarely 'see by the light of death' because we fear the passing of time and we constantly miss the richness of the world in the pursuit of temporary security and shallow esteem. The escape from our cavern depends upon our becoming conscious of our self-imposed captivity; it depends upon the experience of a guilt which seeks to open up the future, not to linger over past failures, a guilt which makes us long to reach out to others, not to turn in upon ourselves. This is the guilt which can lead to grace because it tells us what we *might* be, if only we will seek to break open the shell of our subjectivity.

Outside the dark cavern of our self-absorption there flows a mighty river, full of variety, turbulence and change. That river frightens us and we put much effort into hiding from it. We look for bulwarks to our own permanence in our work, possessions, children. We seek to justify ourselves by measuring our achievements against those of others. We like to pretend that, though all else changes, our little hiding place is safe forever. But we cannot really shut our ears to the sound of time's river, which flows all around us, and within our most secret hiding place. The guilt which leads to freedom brings its sound constantly back to our attention. It reminds us of the poverty of our relationships with the people and the things all around us, as we timorously peer at them through the chinks of our cavern; it reminds us of the futility of our efforts to atone for the past, to bargain for the future, to do anything rather than launch out into the turbulence of the ever-flowing present. The heavens declare God's glory (Ps. 19:1); deep calls out to deep, even as the frightening waves break over us (Ps. 42:7); man is crowned with glory and honour in a creation rich in beauty and power (Ps. 8: 3–5). Yet we know only dissatisfaction, boredom, petty self-concern, missing the shining complexity and the awesome depths all around us. Our sin is the sin of Adam: we make ourselves into rival gods, unable to rejoice in God's goodness, unable to accept our limitations, missing our true peace, hiding from his glory.

GRACE AND GRACEFULNESS

If such is the cavern of sin, how may pastoral care bring about liberation and a joyful welcoming of God's goodness and glory? The question is not easily answered, for the release from sin which we call grace comes in surprising ways, often when we least expect it and from the most unlikely sources. Certainly the Christian churches have frequently tried to make themselves into the official dispensers of this liberating power. Thus the Sacrament of Penance (whether public or private) is an attempt to create a structure within which specific sins can be identified, contrition expressed and ab-

72

solution authoritatively declared; and in the prayers of confession in public worship an opportunity is provided for each individual to recognize his sinfulness and to seek the remedy for his guilt. Such ritualized searches for release from guilt undoubtedly bring peace and 'time for amendment of life' to many people, but we must not suppose that they are the only way in which grace can be received by the guilt-ridden. If we do, we fall prey to an 'ecclesiastical imperialism' which attempts to deny the working of God's Spirit in all human life. Each of us has a pastorhood to offer to others: each of us, therefore, can be 'instruments of God's peace' to another. But this is not to be achieved by making everyone into priests or preachers! Rather, it means a more adventurous exploration of what it might mean to speak of grace *incarnate*, grace embodied in our humanity. Another way of expressing it is to ask what it might mean to be a person who is 'graceful' – who is a body characterized by grace.

Embodiment
We saw earlier the danger of an approach to guilt which merely underwrites the authority of an externally imposed moralistic conscience. The guilt which prepares for grace must open up people's vision, not bully them into a submissive obedience; it must help restore them to their rightful place in the glory of the universe, not create a personality ridden with strife, anxiety and a sense of worthlessness. Grace is the entering of God's Spirit into the temple which is our body (1 Cor. 6:19): guilt makes that temple ready, grace hallows it. Therefore when we speak of the mediation of grace we are not describing some extra-terrestial event, some mysterious transaction involving a disembodied soul. On the contrary, grace is always God's *embodiment*, the creation of a harmony between body and spirit for which the adjective 'graceful' is a supremely appropriate description. The person who is freed from sin's cavern feels at home in the swirling beauty of creation; he moves gracefully at last, no longer at war within himself, no longer an alien in God's world.

Such embodiment of grace is at the heart of the Christian gospel, giving it that earthiness which both attracts and scandalizes us. The apparently shameful pregnancy of Mary is hailed by the angel as God's gracing of her body; John the Baptist's testimony to the Messiah begins as a joyous leap in

73

his mother's womb; an old man takes the infant Jesus in his arms and finds grace in his last days:

> Lord, now lettest thou thy servant depart in peace,
> according to thy word:
> For mine eyes have seen thy salvation,
> Which thou hast prepared before the face of all people;
> A light to lighten the Gentiles,
> and the glory of thy people Israel.
>
> (Luke 2: 29–32 AV)

Here we see examples of *bodies* mediating grace. It is Mary's female body which allows her to be recipient of grace; John's nascent life which spontaneously heralds that grace; Simeon's ageing eyes which see the dawning of the light of grace in a tiny child. Such strange transformations of ordinary bodily events should give us courage. Could *our* bodies too be the vehicles of grace? Could the physical nature of our bodies and the growth from infancy to old age of our bodies contain such gracefulness? Following the leads suggested by the experience of Mary, John and Simeon, I wish to suggest that liberation from sin can be embodied in the gracefulness of our sexuality and the gracefulness of our age.

Sexuality and Gracefulness

In the Christian tradition sexuality has been regarded as the last place in which grace is to be found. The elevation of virginity and celibacy above the married state and the fear and distrust of the 'lust' entailed in sexual intercourse led to the equation of sexuality with sin. Physical sexual characteristics came to be seen as distasteful aspects of man's animal nature and sexual attraction as an unfortunate necessity for the continuation of the species, to be resisted by the spiritually strong.[15] (Thus Luther could describe marriage as 'a hospital for incurables, which prevents its inmates from falling into graver sin'!)[16] Such negative views of sexuality are now virtually universally rejected by Christian theologians, and the churches have come to emphasize the blessings of marriage and the positive contribution of sexual pleasure to the marital relationship. Yet still much of the gracefulness of sexuality is overlooked, and the relevance of this gracefulness to every person, young or old, married or single is rarely discussed.

Rather than viewing sexuality solely in the context of phys-

74

ical acts (love play, intercourse, masturbation, etc.) we need to recognize it as 'a radiance pervading every human relationship, but assuming a particular intensity at certain points'.[17] The radiance of sexuality consists in the pleasurable awareness of possessing a body which is either male or female and the joyful recognition of the maleness and femaleness of others. (The importance of this recognition of sexuality for our sense of identity is dramatically illustrated by the dilemma of the transsexual who, although possessing a body with the physical characteristics of one sex, feels convinced that he or she is really a member of the opposite sex.)[18] Such radiance is often markedly absent in those who are sexually active and clearly present in those who have chosen celibacy or who for other reasons do not express their sexuality in physical acts. Sexuality is graceful when it coheres in the life of the individual possessing it, when it enhances the quality of all his relationships.[19] (Thus the sexually active person can still be sexually frustrated, in the sense that his sexual behaviour fails to fulfill him as a person. Such a person does not know the gracefulness of sex.)

A further dimension of sexuality will enable us to see its liberating potential more clearly. The physical differentiation between male and female though distinctive (except in a few genetically abnormal individuals)[20] is by no means absolute. Anatomically and genetically each sex contains the rudiments of the typical features of the opposite sex and when the hormone balance is altered 'masculinization' or 'feminization' can occur. It may therefore be more correct to describe an individual as *predominately* male or *predominately* female, in a physical sense. This must lead us to be highly suspicious of any sexual stereotyping which inhibits the full range of our emotional relationships to ourselves and others. C. G. Jung (although still caught in many old-fashioned stereotypes of manhood and womanhood) was one of the first to see the inhibiting effect of an insistence on a sharp emotional differentiation between the sexes:

No man is so entirely masculine that he has nothing feminine in him. The fact is, rather, that very masculine men have carefully guarded and hidden a very soft emotional life often incorrectly described as 'feminine'. A man counts it a virtue to repress his feminine traits as much as possible,

75

just as a woman, at least until recently, considered it unbecoming to be 'mannish'.[21]

The gracefulness of sexuality consists in discovering the rich complexity which a blend of maleness and femaleness offers us. We can rejoice in the differences and rejoice in the sameness, not afraid of the 'sexual revolution' of our time, since it offers to men and women alike an amazing range of self-expression. Sexuality is graceful because it helps us to trust God's creation, venturing forth, as James B. Nelson's words suggest, to a place of music:

> We are . . . unique individuals, female and male, each with the capacity to be both firm and tender, receiving and giving, rational and intuitive, diffused in awareness and focused in thinking, flexible and strong – like a duet in which two instruments skilfully blend into harmonious oneness.[22]

Against this background we can begin to see the needs of the guilt-ridden in a different light. To overcome their alienation, their self-absorption, they need an embodiment of grace – the warm sexuality of another's presence. Such a view of pastoral care is easily misunderstood and distorted! It must not be confused with the exploitative seductiveness with which sexually frustrated people sometimes offer care to others. (Such seductiveness comes from the helper's own need and sense of sexual inadequacy.) Rather, the helper's presence is sexual simply because it truly is *bodily* presence, not some formalized and distancing ritual. To refer back to the imagery of previous chapters: the helper's presence has the wholesome closeness and courage of the shepherd, the openness and vulnerability of the wounded healer, the simplicity and laughable humanity of the fool.

Inevitably, then, the helper in bringing himself to the guilty person brings his sexuality. To assist in the other's liberation, this sexual presence must be graceful. One of the most remarkable stories in the Gospels is Luke's description of a woman ('who lived a sinful life'), wetting Jesus' feet with her tears, drying them with her hair, then kissing and anointing them (Luke 7:36–50). The story describes an intimacy which horrified the Pharisee, in whose house Jesus was a guest. Yet this is not a story of seduction, but of grace. Jesus welcomes

76

her physical expressions of love, because he knows their meaning. Jesus does not deny his masculinity and shrink from the touch of this 'sinful' woman: he uses his masculinity as an instrument of grace: 'Your faith has saved you; go in peace.'

As we slowly emerge from the long history of male domination of the ministry, of denial of sexuality within the churches and of a formalized and defensive style of pastoral care, we can hope for some acceptance of such gracefulness of sexuality in both those who offer and those who receive pastoral care. This will not be easy to achieve, since we are speaking of a subtle balance of body and spirit which is often destroyed by our fears and our insensitivity. Thus the increasingly important role of women in the churches could help to enrich the sexuality of care; but if the women feel constrained to emulate and compete with the men, then the femininity they might offer will be denied. If, as I suggested earlier, there is a music in our sexuality then we might see the liberation of the guilt-ridden as a kind of dance. We frequently use the term 'graceful' of dancers, for in them we see a remarkably free use of the body, one which both celebrates it and transcends it. Yet the dancer's freedom comes from learning the art of control: neither spirit denying body, nor body denying spirit, but the wholeness of embodied spirit, a living acceptable offering to the Lord of the Dance. Such is the pastoral care which liberates us from sin's cavern.

Age and Gracefulness

Important as sexual awareness is to us, it is only one of several ways in which our embodiment makes itself known. We are conscious of ourselves not only as male or female, but as tall or short, fat or thin, strong or weak, attractive or unattractive, well co-ordinated or clumsy, and so on. Obviously these evaluations of our bodily state are somewhat arbitrary and subjective, depending upon comparisons with the norms of our social group and upon our estimations of how others perceive us. However, one other aspect of embodiment seems more on a par with sexuality, in the sense of having an objective reference – our age. We are moment by moment embodiments of change through time, bodies at a certain point in the progression from birth to death. Arguably, then, age, like sexuality, has a central part to play in the embodiment of grace in our lives.

As we examine the notion of age more carefully we discover that it is just as subtle and complex as sexuality. Of course, in a simple physical sense, the age of any particular human body is not in doubt; it has lived for a given length of time, beginning with the formation of its first genetically unique cell at conception. But the *meaning* of age to the person who is that body is a different matter. As self-consciousness develops in the growing child he quickly learns to build into his awareness an interpretation of his body's age. This interpretation is nearly always a negative one. The child learns that he is 'too young'. His bodily age means incapacity and the prohibition of things he wants to do. He therefore longs to be older, to enter the privileged adult world. Yet when, in adolescence, that cherished goal is in sight, a strong sense of anxiety is often felt. The adolescent wants to be some other age than his present one, but he cannot decide whether to be younger or to be older is less to be desired! The same ambivalence often characterizes adult years. To be older perhaps means more power and authority, but the price to be paid may be heavier responsibilities and a loss of youthful vigour. As the body continues to age the person may increasingly be tempted to look back, feeling too old already and fearing the disabilities ahead. Now he is prone to give advice to the young:

> 'Remember your Creator in the days of your youth, before evil days come and the years approach when you say, "These give me no pleasure." '
>
> (Eccles. 12:1 JB)

As disability increases and death approaches, there may be moments of great bitterness at opportunities missed and friendships broken, and a sense of being uncared for, of being 'on the scrap heap' of society.

No doubt this is too gloomy a picture of how age may be interpreted, but such a constant negation of our body's age is increasingly common, and is aggravated by modern society's pre-occupation with youthful vigour and physical allure. We all have a tendency to avoid encounter with present reality by living either in fantasies about the future or in highly selective memories of the past.[23] In terms of the imagery I used earlier, we find it hard to move with the river. Our fantasies and our memories provide temporary islands for us where we can close our ears to the rushing water and pretend that nothing changes. But our islands cannot withstand the river's power, and when finally its current sweeps us along with the undeniable onset of old age we feel panic and despair. Yet it need not be like this, if we learn to welcome age as a grace.

Since we believe in incarnate love, in grace embodied in the man Jesus, we should learn to look for that grace at all stages of human growth and development. The gospel narratives tell us virtually nothing of the life of Jesus before the short period of ministry leading to his death. However, the incident reported in Luke's Gospel of the twelve year old Jesus in discussion with the teachers in the Temple is suggestive of what I mean by gracefulness in age. There is an unabashed wisdom in such young children which saves them from being ignored and discredited as too young to understand. They are not necessarily precocious, 'old for their years'. They are simply not cowed by the adult insistence that they should know their place. (What could possibly be said in response to the calm question: 'Why did you have to look for me? Didn't you know that I had to be in my Father's house?' (Luke 2:49 TEV)?) In the same way old Eli shows his wisdom when he realizes that it is the Lord who is speaking to the boy Samuel (1 Sam. 3:1–18), awakening the simple responsiveness of the child, as he sleeps in the darkened sanctuary. In the words of the Psalmist, the praise of God can come even from babies, from infants suckled at the breast (Ps. 8:2). Adult wisdom is not always so wise, after all!

Yet the point of speaking of the gracefulness of age is not to elevate any *one* age above another (whether we are describing the wisdom of the young Jesus or of the aged Simeon who earlier had cradled him in his arms). Rather, it is to see the beauty and the potentiality of *any* age. The secret lies in refusing to allow the age to dominate the person: the person must be freed to express himself through the medium of his age. So there are infant voices and aged voices, youthful voices and mature voices, voices of adolescence and voices of middle age; and all have their own gracefulness, if we will let them speak. It is curiously difficult for us to realize this. In some societies the superiority of the elders is stressed to such an extent that younger people must always bow to their authority. In other more 'developed' societies the stress is all on the younger more active members, with an equal disregard for the contribution of the very young and the very old. Thus people learn to be discontent with their age for most of their lives, and to ignore those who are not at the 'ideal' age for the society.

We see then once more the need for liberation, if people are to trust in the goodness of God's time, rather than to be trapped in the discontent of those who live alternately for the future and for the past. It is in the embodiment of age's gracefulness that pastoral care will meet this need. As with sexuality, so with age, the traditional ministry of the churches has had difficulty in mediating gracefulness of this kind. The difficulty originates in the stress on rationality and on maturity which the *teaching* ministry of the Church requires. Naturally such a stress produces as a norm the person in the middle years of life, mature enough to know what he is talking about, not so old that he is losing his intellectual grip. But such middle-aged people are by no means necessarily the best embodiments of gracefulness in age! Often the very old, living calmly in proximity to death, can bring that release from the fear of time which the guilty person needs. Often again the lively young person, full of faith in the present and of joy in new experience, is the one who restores courage to others in their pointless battle with time. The middle-aged person (often the one who is given most responsibility for caring) is least naturally suited to be the instrument of such grace. Men and women at this age have to learn to accept the transition from youthful energy to the quieter pace of old age. Caught in this inward struggle, they often find it difficult to 'grow old gracefully' and so become resentful of younger people and impatient with older ones. Their faces show the strain and their bodies the tenseness of people for whom time is an enemy not a friend, and they mediate grace*lessness*, for all their efforts to care.

Yet, paradoxically, those who have the greatest struggle with ageing have the potential to become the best helpers of others. We recall yet again the images of caring in the earlier chapters: the shepherd who knows the fear of the dark valley; the healer who has acknowledged his own wounds; the fool who makes a butt of his own simplicity. In the last analysis, we shall not help others if we have never experienced their fear of change, have never needed to ask for help ourselves when the tumult of the river is more than we can bear. We give to others only what we have received ourselves, through the mediation of God's grace from fellow travellers in time. If we move gracefully in that river for the present, if our faces show some serenity and our bodies can relax despite the frightening current, it is only because through the agency of another, on that same voyage to our body's death, we have found the utter calmness of the Lord of Time: 'I am the Alpha and the Omega, the beginning and the end, the first and the last' (Rev. 22:13 AV).

7

The Journey

Footfalls echo in the memory
Down the passage which we did not take
Towards the door we never opened
Into the rose garden.

T. S. Eliot, *Burnt Norton*[1]

We come finally to the problem of faith. The mystery of our lives is not as easily solved as we might think in those heady moments when the joy of liberating grace fills our hearts. Certainly grace opens a new vision, gives fresh courage. Yet the problem of faith remains. Our lives continue through many difficulties and uncertainties, and the struggle to make sense of it all goes on: 'We wait for God to make us his sons and set our whole being free' (Rom. 8:23 TEV). So faith often falters and the bright hope coming from our moments of release from sin's cavern can seem like an empty dream. For this reason, traditional pastoral care has always stressed the need to nourish and strengthen faith throughout a person's life. Each of us has a pilgrimage to make on a road which is strangely familiar, though we know we have never trodden it before. We find ourselves on a journey, beginning at birth, ending at death, whose destination we only dimly understand. We know we are searching for something, yet the nature of the thing we seek constantly eludes us. On this strange journey, in this tantalizing search, we often feel lonely and bemused, in need of guidance, encouragement, companionship. Not always knowing what we are asking, we reach out for the help of others to lead us back to faith.

JOURNEYING AND SEARCHING

As we begin to think more carefully about this problem we shall realize that metaphors like 'searching' or 'journeying' are somewhat inadequate for describing the quest for faith. There are senses in which faith can never be found by a search, however persistent, nor reached by a journey, however long. As we shall see later in this chapter, our strivings and wanderings are often the biggest impediments to faith. Faith comes when we cease our restless quest for it. Faith is the beginning, as well as the end, of the journey. Yet, paradoxically, the journey and the search are also part of the experience. Only in movement do we experience the repose of faith, just as it is only against the dark that we can perceive light. I shall begin, therefore, by considering the quest for faith as a journey, using as illustrations two very different accounts of such journeys: Hermann Hesse's *Siddhartha* and John Bunyan's *Pilgrim's Progress*.

Two Journeys

Hesse's novel, *Siddhartha*, is a work of great literary power and beauty, written in language at once simple and majestic. The summary which I offer must therefore deprive the book of much of its poetic force and will be a poor substitute for the insight which the author offers. But it is a work of such importance in understanding the nature of a life search that the risk must be taken of doing it a grave injustice by making it appear prosaic.

The central character of the novel is Siddhartha, the son of an Indian Brahmin, who finds that he must leave the serene and holy atmosphere of his father's home in search of an inner peace and truth. He leaves home with his friend Govinda and their search takes them first to the forests to become Samanas (wandering ascetics) and at length to a grove where they meet the Buddha and hear him teach. Govinda becomes a disciple of the Buddha, but Siddhartha cannot find there the peace he is seeking. He leaves Govinda and journeys on to a city where he meets the beautiful courtesan, Kamala. Siddhartha successfully woos Kamala, takes up employment with a merchant and quickly becomes skilled in the arts of sexual love and of business. Yet still he finds no peace. One day he flees the city and in a state of exhaustion reaches a river bank and the hut of a ferryman. The ferryman teaches him to ply the ferry, and at last Siddhartha seems to be finding himself. But one day Kamala comes to the river bank and is killed before his eyes. He discovers that she has borne him a son, but the boy rebels against Siddhartha and runs away, leaving him once more alone with the ferryman and the river. This final pain is at last transcended by Siddhartha when he learns (at the ferryman's gentle urging) to listen to the river:

> Siddhartha saw the river hasten, made up of himself and his relations and all the people he had ever seen. All the waves and water hastened, suffering, towards goals, many goals, to the waterfall, to the sea, to the current, to the ocean and all goals were reached and each one was succeeded by another. The water changed to vapour and rose, became rain and came down again, became spring, brook and river, changed anew, flowed anew. But the yearning voice had altered. It still echoed sorrowfully, searchingly but other voices accompanied it, voices of pleasure and sorrow, good and evil voices, laughing and lamenting voices, hundreds of voices, thousands of voices.
>
> Siddhartha listened. . . . He could no longer distinguish the different voices – the merry voice from the weeping voice, the childish voice from the manly voice. They all belonged to each other; the lament of those who yearn, the laughter of the wise, the cry of indignation and groan of the dying. They were all interwoven and interlocked, entwined in a thousand ways. And all the voices, all the goals, all the yearnings, all the sorrows, all the pleasures, all the good and evil, all of them together was the world. All of them together was the stream of events, the music of life.[2]

Now Siddhartha finds the inner peace he had been seeking so long:

> From that hour Siddhartha ceased to fight against his destiny. There shone in his face the serenity of knowledge, of one who is no longer confronted with conflict of desires, who has found salvation, who is in harmony with the stream of events, with the stream of life, full of sympathy

and compassion, surrendering himself to the stream, belonging to the unity of all things.[3]

We enter a very different world in John Bunyan's *Pilgrim's Progress*. True, Bunyan's pilgrim, Christian, also engages in a search and undertakes an eventful journey before he eventually reaches the Celestial City. Christian also comes to a river at journey's end, but this is a river which must be crossed once in order to reach the gates of the city on the other side. Christian leaves this world for another at the end of his journey: Siddhartha becomes one with the world, 'belonging to the unity of all things'. Moreover, on Christian's journey good and evil are starkly contrasted. Christian runs into many perils: the Slough of Despond, Vanity Fair, Doubting Castle and its owner, Giant Despair; and has no difficulty in seeing them as dangers (though this does not prevent his nearly being enslaved by them). Siddhartha, on the other hand, must forsake things which are outwardly good – his father's love and piety, the holy life of the Samanas, the serenity of the Buddha's grove – and must learn from more 'worldly' things: the commerce of the city, the sexual joys of Kamala's love, the experience of having wealth and power. But perhaps the clearest contrast of all is between the different portrayals by Bunyan and Hesse of companionship on the journey. Christian constantly encounters two sharply contrasted classes of companion: those who will distract him and try to dissuade him from his pilgrimage (Obstinate, Pliable, Worldly-Wise, Talkative and many others), and those who guide him and support him through the perils and temptations (Evangelist, Interpreter, Faithful, Hopeful). Siddhartha's companions, on the other hand, are not so obviously good or bad and they all contribute something to his search: Govinda, his friend who chooses the orthodox way, Kamala, the prostitute, Kamaswami, the merchant, Vasudeva, the ferryman. Each helps Siddhartha in his journey to peace. Yet finally that journey is also one which Siddhartha must make *alone*. Siddhartha's journey is what Dag Hammarskjöld called 'the longest journey', the journey into self.[4]

Teaching and Learning

We see, then, that these two accounts of journeys are written from very different perspectives. Bunyan writes in the confidence that the route and the destination are already clearly known. Deviations from the true path come only from the pilgrim's own foolishness and weakness. The path itself is made abundantly plain to him by trustworthy guides and companions. Hesse, on the other hand, is describing not only a journey but a *search*. Siddhartha must find the path for himself and no one can know what that path will be until he himself treads it. Siddhartha's companions are important to him certainly, but often in ways they do not themselves realize.

This contrast takes us to the heart of the puzzle of teaching and learning. In *Philosophical Fragments*, Søren Kierkegaard has exposed the problem with his usual ironical brilliance. He quotes Socrates' account of the difficulty in the *Meno*: How can the truth be learned? For either one knows it already, in which case one need not seek it; or one does not know it, in which case one cannot even know for what to seek.[5] This is precisely the difficulty left by the contrasting journeys of Christian and Siddhartha. If the sign-posts on the route are as clear as Bunyan implies, how could anyone possibly lose the way? If they are as elusive as Hesse implies, how does anyone ever manage to *find* the way? Kierkegaard's answer to the Socratic paradox is that, in order for man to know the truth, God must create the condition in him that will make this possible. Yet God must do this in a way that leaves man free, for otherwise he is merely threatened or cajoled into a semblance of the truth. (This would seem to be precisely the danger of the terrors and joys so graphically described by Bunyan.) Kierkegaard concludes that it is through taking the humble form of a servant that God makes it possible for man to know him and love him and so to be in the condition for finding the truth: 'For this is the unfathomable nature of love, that it desires equality with the beloved, not in jest merely, but in earnest and truth.'[6]

If we adopt Kierkegaard's solution to the paradox we are bound to conclude that God alone is capable of being a teacher in matters of faith, for he alone can create the necessary condition for learning. Thus Kierkegaard rejects the idea that the contemporaries of Jesus were in any privileged position in relation to faith. (For, as he points out, many saw and heard Jesus and did *not* follow him.)[7] Each generation and each individual is unique; each has the same possibility

86

of discipleship or the lack of it; each must gain the condition for learning from God alone. (Later generations inherit the *testimony* of the apostolic generation; but whether they respond to that testimony in faith remains a matter between them and God.)[8]

Such a view leaves little room for pastoral care as teaching: *I* cannot know the right way for another; *I* cannot create in him the condition for learning; *I* cannot be his teacher, guide or saviour. This seems to me a correct conclusion at the fundamental level of how each individual person makes his life's journey. No human being can fully enter the life of another or live it for him. Yet this need not prevent us asking what it might mean to be a *companion* of another on his life's journey (and to have others as companions on ours). A companion does not necessarily know the way any better than we do. But he shares the journey with us for a while and helps us as best he can with his own limited love and vision. In order to understand what such companionship could mean we shall look first in more detail at the nature of people's life searches.

LIFE SEARCHES

In using the term 'life search' I am attempting to describe those fundamental goals in terms of which people organize their day to day living. (Paul Tillich's distinction between 'proximate' and 'ultimate' concerns is a way of exploring this same idea.)[9] Frequently we are only dimly aware of having such goals and, of course, much of our behaviour is inconsistent with them, or contradictory in the sense of trying to pursue two incompatible goals at once. Nevertheless, because human beings possess awareness of the flow of time from birth to death, they can scarcely avoid engaging in a 'life search' of one kind or another.

In recent psychological theory there has developed a school of thought which has attempted to describe these goal-directed aspects of human behaviour in terms of the development of the ego, or sense of identity. (One of its main proponents, Abraham H. Maslow, has named the school the 'Third Force', to distinguish it from Psychoanalysis on the one side and Behaviourism on the other.)[10] These theorists consider that attempts to explain all human behaviour simply as the out-come of psychological drives (for example, the 'Pleasure Principle' of early Freudian theory) are bound to fail. Human beings have 'self-actualization' needs which demand a different kind of satisfaction from the simple tension release of bodily-based needs. The 'higher needs' require the achievement of a sense of meaning and purpose in life. I shall briefly summarize two 'self-actualization' theories of this type: Maslow's account of the hierarchy of human needs and Erikson's description of ego-identity and the life cycle.

In the writings of A. H. Maslow[12] human behaviour is regarded as the outcome of two basic opposing forces: Defence and Growth. (In his later works Maslow prefers the terms, Deficiency-motivation and Being-motivation.) Many of the strongest human needs are concerned with the defence of the organism: hunger, thirst, maintenance of body temperature, shelter, safety, etc.; but when these needs are reasonably satisfied, human beings then seek other goals: group identity, the gaining of prestige and power, and self-expression through creative activities of various kinds. In order for there to be growth (in a psychological sense), the need for creativity and self-expression must be given some outlet; but if the 'lower' needs are too much neglected, the drive for safety will reassert itself and the individual will direct his behaviour towards bodily comfort, a sense of belongingness and social prestige. Thus one sees an oscillation between Defence and Growth in people's lives, one which varies from individual to individual and from time to time. For the majority of people a *hierarchy of need* operates whereby the 'lower needs' of bodily comfort and social esteem receive most satisfaction, while the 'higher' self-actualization needs emerge only occasionally and are only partially satisfied.

In his later writings Maslow has concentrated on these higher self-actualization needs, paying particular attention to what he calls 'peak experience'. Peak experiences are 'transient moments of self-actualization. They are moments of ecstasy which cannot be bought, cannot be guaranteed, cannot even be sought.'[13] Maslow believes that such experiences are really quite common, though they are often ignored. People who do pay attention to them are self-actualizing people, or 'peakers'. They are 'without one single exception, involved in a cause outside their own skin, in something outside of themselves.'[14]

Thus Maslow's theories provide a description of various forms of life search. For many people 'Deficiency-motivation' predominates. They devote their energies to making themselves financially and materially secure and to gaining self-esteem through recognition by others. Threats to these guarantees of their security make them feel anxious and vulnerable, because they possess no inner certainty of their own worth. Others have a powerful need to be loved. They cling to personal relationships and place great importance on popularity and social success. They *need* these relationships in order to feel safe and they devote their lives to creating and maintaining them. Others again seem relatively free from such 'Deficiency-motivation'. Although material security, prestige and popularity may hold some limited importance for them, their most powerful motivation is toward the pursuit of some value (beauty, truth, service of others) and their life-search is organized around this pursuit. A final implication of Maslow's theory is that those people who organize their life on the basis of Deficiency–motivation will eventually experience a profound sense of inner dissatisfaction because of the neglect of their creative, self-actualizing capacities.[15]

We may now turn to a second psychological theory, that of Erik Erikson, to add the dimension of time to the concept of life search. According to Erikson the individual's personal identity (or 'ego') develops through a series of stages beginning at infancy and continuing to old age. He identifies eight such stages, each one characterized by a particular crisis or turning-point.[16] The earliest crisis, occurring in the first months of the infant's life, is that of 'trust v. mistrust' and the degree to which the infant feels secure (possesses 'basic trust') will influence the outcome of the seven subsequent crises which are: autonomy v. shame and doubt; initiative v. guilt; industry v. inferiority; identity v. role confusion; intimacy v. isolation; generativity v. stagnation; and integrity v. despair. Erikson does *not* believe that all human action is wholly causally determined[17] but he does assert that the 'nexus of psychological and social forces' operating at these various critical turning-points will show their effects in the individual's development. In particular, the patterns of child-rearing in any given culture will create in each person major motivating forces which will be operative all his life. At adolescence especially, the earlier crises (trust, autonomy, initiative and industry) reappear and exert a powerful influence on the formation of the adult identity.

As with Maslow, we can find in Erikson ideas which give content to the concept of a life search. People often carry with them into adult life the unresolved conflicts of childhood. Legacies of mistrust, shame, guilt and feelings of inferiority lead them to attempt to prove themselves in various ways. Money, power, prestige, sexual relationships, family, career, friendships can all be used as means towards lessening the sense of earlier loss or failure. Yet (as Erikson also observes) the approach of old age with its awareness of eventual death reveals the inadequacy of such temporary solutions. At this point in a person's life some sense of integrity, of a meaning which both gives shape to and transcends the individual's life, is needed, if he is not to give way to despair and disgust.[18] The final life search is one which has to take death into account. Thus Erikson believes that a culture which has learned to face death is the one which best helps people to live and grow: '. . . healthy children will not fear life if their elders have integrity enough not to fear death.'[19]

FAITH AND COMPANIONSHIP

We have now seen, with the aid of Maslow and Erikson, something of the needs of people as they journey through life. Like Bunyan's pilgrim they are threatened by the Slough of Despond, by Vanity Fair, by Giant Despair. Like Hesse's wandering Brahmin they stumble from place to place in pursuit of an elusive peace, wavering between self-denial and self-indulgence in an effort to find themselves. Theorists like Maslow and Erikson strain psychological categories to breaking point in describing such life searches, because they are trying to describe something beyond psychology – the state of transcendence we call faith. It is one thing to point to the 'beyond' in the midst of life, call it 'peak experience', 'ego integrity' or what we will: it is quite another to explain how it comes about in any person's life. At times it seems within our grasp, but then it eludes us once more.

Nothing could be more arrogant than to suggest that we

90

ourselves have finally 'arrived' on this journey of faith – unless it is to set ourselves up as the expert route-finders for others! Of course we can often see when we (and others) have gone wrong, have wandered off the way that leads to our true peace. But to *find* the way again (not in outward conformity, but in inner truth), that is infinitely harder. I have already suggested that the idea of companionship may be the best means of describing that subtle relationship of caring which opens the way back to faith. I shall now suggest three modes of such companionship: sharing bread on the road to faith; sharing repose in the midst of the journey; sharing danger at journey's end.

Sharing Bread

The root meaning of 'companion' is 'he who shares bread'. This has significance at several levels. At the simplest level it means that we are one with others in our fellow humanity. Like them, we must eat to live and, even in the most sophisticated of us, the fight for survival is only a little below the surface. It is out of this knowledge of fear and fragility that we support the other in word and action when faith seems far away. If we manage to speak to his fear it is because we know it ourselves and make ourselves no better than he in pointing it out. If we manage to comfort his sense of loss, it is only because the loss strikes to our heart and starts tears in our eyes. Thus companionship is a way of understanding why people get caught up with 'proximate' goals, with the temporary security of popularity, fame, success. But the good companion also knows, in his own experience that 'man does not live by bread alone' (Deut. 8:3; Mat. 4:4). He has found in his own life the living bread (John 6:51), the bread from a loving Father freely given if only we will ask for it (Mat. 7:9), the bread broken in love for us (Mat. 26:26). So the good companion 'shares bread' in the sense that he helps people to transcend the anxiety about material things, which can ultimately give them no peace. The essential *equality* of companionship must remain however. As soon as a needy person senses he is being viewed from a vantage point of spiritual superiority, from the smugness of a faith without doubt, he will feel once more alone in his search. In an often quoted phrase of the evangelist D. T. Niles, the message of faith is no more than one starving man telling another where bread is to be found.

At a second level, the 'sharer of bread' enters the other's life for a while. The companion is more than a chance acquaintance. He interrupts his own preoccupations and pitches in his lot with the other. Perhaps the companionship lasts only a short space of time, but while it lasts the companion *shares* with the other. He is not present in body but absent in spirit, or the companionship is merely superficial. On the journey of faith a companion gives something of himself to the other; so much so, that when the time comes to go separate ways again (however necessary that may be) there will be a sense of regret. The absence as well as the presence of a companion has significance.[20] Yet the true companion is also someone who avoids making himself indispensable to the other or becoming parasitic on the other. This again must be true in words and in actions. We can only share in someone else's life search if we are prepared to expose ourselves a little, speaking about things which matter deeply to us as well as the other and risking ourselves in service of the other. But our companionship fails if our words dominate *his* search or if our actions remove *his* need to journey on.

At a third level 'sharing bread' denotes a communion which sustains and transcends the companionship. All discipleship of Jesus is companionship in this sense. As Jesus shared bread with his disciples, so he told them to remember him with the same common sharing (1 Cor. 11:24f). He told his disciples that only two or three needed to be present in his name for him to be present also (Mat. 18:20). The small numbers are significant, when we consider the personal closeness of companionship. (It seems a great impoverishment of this personal sharing that companionship and communion have been split apart through the ritualization of the latter, so that people who are strangers to one another – and intend to remain so – 'share Communion'.) The fellow humanity and mutual sharing of companionship open the way for the presence of Christ. The stranger on the Emmaus road, the guest at the table, the one who joins our search for truth in all the puzzlement and contradiction of the events of our lives becomes Christ present (Luke 24:13–35). Such companionship is not to be confused with an anxious seeking out of the company of the like-minded in order to protect ourselves from too challenging a confrontation in life. The true companion often begins as a stranger. In giving a welcome to such strangers we may entertain angels unawares (Heb. 13:2), for, in the words of St Patrick, we shall often find Christ 'in the mouth of friend *and* stranger'.

Sharing Repose

Companionship is also the sharing of repose. The person who seeks companionship on faith's journey is often unaware that his greatest need is for a friend who will refuse to take his anxious striving too seriously. The companion, who is also a good friend, is capable of mediating that atmosphere of faith so well described in a sermon of Paul Tillich's:

> It is as though a voice were saying: 'You are accepted, *you are accepted*, accepted by that which is greater than you, and the name of which you do not know. Do not ask for the name now. Perhaps you will find it later. Do not try to do anything now. Perhaps later you will do much. Do not seek for anything, do not perform anything. Do not intend anything. Simply accept the fact that you are accepted.'[21]

The essential thing about all friendship is that it puts a different value on time. There is no such thing as being *efficient* at friendship (not genuine friendship), since it is not an activity which aims at achieving something. A friend helps me to share the joy of the moment, creates treasures for my memory and joyful anticipation for my future. Although my friends and I may do things together, the heart of friendship is a *way of being*, not any particular activity. Thus friendship alters the rhythms of time, introducing a cross-rhythm to the onward drives of purpose and desire. Friendship is a sharing of the joy of doing nothing.

In a poem rich with images of repose, Rabindranath Tagore describes a journey in which the haste of his fellow-travellers is in sharp contrast with the restfulness all around:

> The sun rose to the mid sky and doves cooed in the shade. Withered leaves danced and whirled in the hot air of noon. The shepherd boy drowsed and dreamed in the shadow of the banyan tree, and I laid myself down by the water and stretched my tired limbs on the grass.
> My companions laughed at me in scorn; they held their

heads high and hurried on; they never looked back nor rested; they vanished in the distant blue haze. . . .

Deserted by his restless companions, the poet finds that in letting go, in ceasing from striving, he has in fact come to his journey's end:

> The repose of the sun-embroidered gloom slowly spread over my heart. I forgot for what I had travelled, and I surrendered my mind without struggle to the maze of shadows and songs.

> At last, when I woke from my slumber and opened my eyes, I saw thee standing by me, flooding my sleep with thy smile. How I had feared that the path was long and wearisome, and the struggle to reach thee was hard![22]

A striking aspect of Tagore's poem is the sense of restfulness conveyed by the images of nature ('the repose of the sun-embroidered gloom'; 'the maze of shadows and songs'). Like the travellers in the poem, we usually discount rest or repose, regarding it as an interruption of living rather than as part of it. It seems that we cannot resist giving a positive value to activity, and a neutral or even negative value to rest ('inactivity', 'idleness'). Yet it is in moments of repose that we may be most free to learn, for then we no longer filter our experience according to the constraints of some self-centred, driving purpose.[23] Thus repose, the deliberate cessation from activity, can be seen as an important avenue to the life of faith.

The companionship which is also friendship knows the virtue of doing nothing and so freely offers a fellowship of inactivity, an encouragement to repose. The experience of worship (where this has not been corrupted by our anxious activism) provides the pattern for such openings for faith. Worship is sharing time with a friend. The Sabbath which is truly made for man gives him release from his need to work. The day of the Lord's resurrection puts a time of hope and joy at the beginning of every week. The rhythm of the Christian festivals offers release from the treadmill of a life measured by productivity. Praying together, singing together, being silent together, listening together: these components of worship are the sounds and silences of a warm friendship, where 'hearts are open . . . no secrets are hid', where time can be spent with a God who henceforth calls us not servants but friends (John 15:15). Such friendship is often hard to find in long-established churches, in which worship has become an *activity*, sustained out of a sense of obligation to a God who demands regularity. In such places the dusty and disorientated traveller feels ill at ease, an outsider disturbing the stately routine of God's more diligent worshippers. So the friendship of God and the friendship of man must intertwine, and for all of us the repose of true worship comes only when we are able to relax in the company of those who, for a little while at least, have come close to us, shared our journey, sought with us somewhere to rest.

Comradeship at Journey's End
Finally, companionship on the strange journey of faith must at times become *comradeship*. The comrade is needed when mortal danger looms. He stands by my side, facing a darkness which may engulf us both. In the image of the comrade we recall the courage of the shepherd who enters the dark valley, the bleeding of the healer who knows his own mortality, the crazy loyalty of the fool which makes him enter the night's dark storm. Comradeship is needed when the reality of death is too much for us to bear. Even the most courageous, the most trusting and the most faithful of us can find it hard to gaze calmly into the face of death. For death brings such catastrophic losses. It threatens all that is familiar to us: places where we feel at home, the often unnoticed habitation of our own body, the touch and sound of those we love. Death presents faith with its greatest challenge, because it suggests that there is nothing to hope for, nothing to gain in journeying on, when in the end there is only loss, blankness, extinction:

> To-morrow, and to-morrow, and to-morrow
> Creeps in this petty pace from day to day,
> To the last syllable of recorded time;
> And all our yesterdays have lighted fools
> The way to dusty death . . .
>   it is a tale
> Told by an idiot, full of sound and fury
> Signifying nothing. . . .[24]

The companion who sees no such threat in death will be useless as a comrade at journey's end. Faith is not strengthened by the denial of death's enmity, but rather is insidiously weakened, since such denial prepares us poorly for the anger, fear and grief which bereavement and our own mortality bring. We can call death 'kind and gentle' like St Francis, but only because 'Christ the way hath trod', a comrade going ahead into the cold unknown to lead us home.[25] The enmity of death lies in its finality. Whatever lies beyond it, whether it be darkness or light, it means the ending of life as we have always known it. Naturally then we fight it, unwilling to let go of all we know so well:

> A man can tell himself he is satisfied and peaceful; he can say he has no more wants, that he has fulfilled his duty and is ready to leave. But the heart resists, clutching the stones and grass, it implores, 'Stay a little!'[26]

The comrade, then, is a fellow-soldier who helps us fight a common enemy. He does this by taking our anger and our fear with the utmost seriousness,[27] not by making us feel ashamed of such emotions or by offering a 'religious' consolation which denies the affront of death. But the comrade *is* a fighter. He strengthens our determination that death shall not have the final victory. Such determination is needed not only when death is imminent (for, after all, many of us will die suddenly, with no prior warning); rather, it is a confrontation with powers of darkness which is needed throughout our earthly days. When we shrink from such a direct gaze into the face of death, we live half-lives, trivializing human relationships, inhibited from a full expression of our powers by our terror of the unknown. The good comrade on life's journey will not allow us to diminish ourselves with such evasions and useless defences. He calls us to the real battle where the name of Jesus is mightier than any other sovereignty (Eph. 1:21; Phil. 2:10). The comrade (in the language of Ephesians) encourages us to put on God's armour:

> Stand firm, I say. Fasten on the belt of truth; for coat of mail put on integrity; let the shoes on your feet be the gospel of peace, to give you firm footing; and, with all these, take up the great shield of faith. . . . Take salvation for helmet; for sword, take that which the Spirit gives you – the words that come from God.
>
> (Eph. 6:14–17 NEB)

So we return to the notion of integrity, of steadfastness, with which this book began. The need of the helper and the helped are one: in life, in death in the midst of life, we can give and receive care only by discovering those things which alone enable us to stand firm against every threat to faith. The courage which is demanded of us is not the fearlessness of the person who trusts in his own physical, mental or emotional strength. The courage to fight the dark powers comes from the integrity of the person who trusts in truth and peace, who reaches out for salvation and faith, whose only weapon against despair is the inspiration of God's spirit. Thus the end of the journey of faith is not, as we often suppose, a stepping out of the world into a disembodied, deathless life. On the contrary, the vanquishing of the powers of darkness, reveals the strangest of all mysteries. The end of our journey has been with us from its very beginning: in our life, in our bodies struggling to find peace in their world, in all our wanderings, searchings, journeyings, we have never been separated from the totality of love, which is God (Rom. 8:37–39). When we enter the combat with death, clad in the armour of God, death's power to annul our lives becomes transformed into a revelation of life's completeness:

> With the drawing of this Love and the voice of this Calling
> We shall not cease from exploration
> And the end of all our exploring
> Will be to arrive where we started
> And know the place for the first time.[28]

8

Paths of Rediscovery

> . . . in order to be true to God and to ourselves
> we must break with the familiar, established and
> secure norms and go off into the unknown.
>
> Thomas Merton, *Contemplative Prayer*[1]

All that I have said in this book has been an attempt to
rekindle the imaginations of those who believe that their vocation as Christians leads to a life of caring for others. I have
been concerned to restore to pastoral care a sense of indebt-
edness to *theological* insights, in an attempt to counterbalance
the over-reliance in contemporary literature on the theories
and terminology of psychology and psychotherapy. Since I
regard the language of theology as nearer to the 'poetic' than
to the 'scientific' view of reality,[2] I have not attempted to
construct a coherent and systematic account of the nature of
pastoral care. Instead, by the use of a number of images of
caring (shepherding, healing through wounds, wise folly), and
of images of the need for care (imprisonment in a cavern,
loneliness on a journey), I have hoped to stimulate fruitful
associations of ideas, encouraging people to use the richness
of their own experience to help others.

Yet the *practical* relevance of all that I have written may
still be far from clear. Unlike many modern textbooks on
pastoral care and counselling, this is not a 'how to do it' book.
I have included very few of the case illustrations and verbatim
interviews so common in such textbooks. My omission of such
material has been quite deliberate. I do not wish to give the
impression that there is an obvious and straightforward ap-
plication of the various ideas about caring which the previous
chapters have explored. If we can regard all education as
directed towards three main objectives, the inculcation of

98

knowledge, the development of skills, the influencing of atti-tudes,[3] then this book has been almost exclusively devoted to the third objective. My concern has been to encourage my readers to experiment with a whole range of styles of relating to others, and to allow their religious beliefs to operate not (as is so often the case) as a restrictive orthodoxy, but as a liberating challenge to their habitual ways of offering care.

Thus the usefulness of this book will depend to a very large extent on the degree to which it provokes the reader into ransacking his own unexplored 'lumber room' of inherited images of faith, in order to rediscover the richness and diver-sity of Christ-like care. No doubt the selection I have made has missed many aspects and misrepresented others, but such deficiencies are not ultimately important, provided the spirit of imaginative rediscovery is maintained. Such rediscovery seems to me to be the centre of faith and its absence the sign of dead conformity to tradition. Thus in my attempts to rediscover pastoral care, I find myself in wholehearted agree-ment with William F. Lynch's understanding of the relation-ship between Christ and the imagination:

> What Christ did was to create in his own person a per-manent propaedeutic for the original and active imagining of men in every generation.[4]

In view of all this, this final chapter will contain few conclu-sions of a strictly practical nature, for this would imply that we can substitute method for imagination, debarring the in-dividual from offering care in his uniquely personal way. However, it is possible to describe, at a very general level, certain 'paths of rediscovery', down which we can direct people in the hope of enabling them to express their capacities for care in ways that are truly helpful to others. Three such paths are described: self-knowledge; sharing; and solitude.

SELF-KNOWLEDGE

Everything that I have said about the nature of care has implied the necessity for the helping person to know himself. Because caring is an interaction in areas of life where helper and helped are *both* vulnerable, the person who claims to care must learn to recognize the intrusive quality of his own needs.

99

He will often be tempted to 'solve' his own problems by immersing himself in the problems of others. To be anxious to help others, is usually primarily to be anxious and only secondarily to be concerned about the others' need![5] When we fail to recognize the self-interest in our offers of care we easily ignore the unfortunate recipient of our attentions, forcing upon him the balms which our own insecurity demands. There are many examples of such exploitation in the name of care:[6] The person who fears the threat of illness and death may seek out the disabled and dying and anxiously seek to comfort and support them; the person unsure of the stability of his own personal relationships may volunteer to advise on the marital and family problems of others; the person haunted by doubts about his own beliefs will demand an audience for his assertions of religious certainty. In such situations the offer of care is really a covert seeking for help. Yet, since the helper's need is unacknowledged, no help can truly be received. Instead of the great strength which the recognition of a mutuality of need can bring, the caring relationship becomes dishonest and ultimately depersonalizing.

This tendency to impose our needs on others makes some kind of training for pastoral work essential. The more we emphasize the need to de-professionalize pastoral care (see Chapter Five above), the greater becomes the danger that those people most willing to be care-givers will be the least well prepared for it. The whole concept of a *voluntary* helper carries overtones of a considerate, self-denying person, willing to go the second mile for the sake of the poor and the needy. (Professional care, in contrast, is more realistic in its approach, seeking some financial reward for the work entailed.) This heroic self-image is the greatest obstacle to developing a pastoral care based on integrity. The Christian who seeks to help others, whether in a voluntary or professional capacity, needs to learn a way of confession which opens his own personality to God. That opening will uncover the mixed motives which make up his desire to be a caring person, and so will enable him to seek help for his own needs, and to keep them 'in the minor key' when listening to the needs of others. Appropriate pastoral training is the encouragement of such acts of confession,[7] in a one-to-one relationship with a 'supervisor,'[8] in a training group, or in private recollection and prayer.

Learning to care through fuller knowledge of self entails a discipline which rarely comes naturally to us. It requires a degree of honesty about ourselves and about others which most conventional social encounters avoid. The Christian churches, despite their emphasis on confession and on loving others, tend to encourage insincerity, the hiding of true motives under a veneer of politeness and social respectability. Thus Christians, although usually highly motivated to offer care, are often the most in need of the discipline of self-examination. Public worship and private prayer can themselves become methods of hiding from aspects of ourselves which we prefer not to see. Thomas Merton describes the consequences of using our religion to gain such 'false peace':

> A method of meditation or a form of contemplation that merely produces the illusion of having 'arrived somewhere' . . . will eventually have to be unlearned in dread – or else we will be confirmed in the arrogance, the impenetrable self-assurance of the Pharisee. . . . We will live 'good lives' that are basically inauthentic, 'good' only so long as they permit us to remain established in our respectable and impermeable identities.[9]

In order to care truly there is really no escape from the dread and the pain of coming out of our hiding place into the full light of God's presence. We must learn to know our fears, our wounds and our foolishness, and to know them in quite specific ways, as we reflect upon recent incidents in our lives when others have sought our help. To help us in this discipline we need a trusted friend who will not let us hide, or a small group in which anything can be freely said. In our private reflection, we need to learn to pray in a way that is intimate, rough and ready, perhaps a little impertinent (if we suppose that God favours politeness!):

> Lord, why did you tell me to love all men, my brothers?
> I have tried, but I come back to you, frightened. . . .
> Lord, I was so peaceful at home.[10]

Without the discipline of self-examination we shall find ourselves battling against unseen and enervating forces in our efforts to do what we regard as our Christian duty. Yet this discipline does not add a fresh load, piling duty upon duty.

The discipline of knowing self frees us to offer a love grounded in our own truth, reaching out to the truth in others.

SHARING

If it is hard to learn to know ourselves, it is obviously even harder to learn to know others. Yet our offers of care are useless if they fail to meet the reality of the other person. In the words of Martin Buber:

> Only when I have to do with another essentially, that is, in such a way that he is no longer a phenomenon of my *I* but instead is my *Thou*, do I experience the reality of speech with another – in the irrefragable genuineness of mutuality.[11]

The ideal of I-Thou encounter which Buber describes seems almost unattainable. Our perception of another's 'reality' depends upon radical selectivity on our part. We pay attention to only a fraction of the input which comes to our brain via the senses, and we are constantly engaged in placing interpretations upon such data in order to build up a picture of reality which suits our immediate purpose.[12] Thus we tend to perceive in others only what we are looking for, in order to confirm some prior schema which we bring with us to this encounter. It is most unusual for us to allow the unique features of others to impinge upon our selective perception of them. Moreover, since we are capable of shifting our attention rapidly from one aspect of consciousness to another, we rarely give other people our full and constant attention. As a person is speaking to us, our attention may flit across memories of the past, plans for the future, other aspects of the present environment; and yet retain sufficient attention to his words to grasp their *general* meaning. Such selective perception and minimal attention are very far removed from 'being present' to the other, as Buber understands it. To 'be present' is to allow the otherness of the other to challenge and confront us, thereby changing our perception of his reality and of our own. We might describe it as truly *hearing* and *seeing* the other for the first time.

All preparation for pastoral care must pave the way for such I-Thou encounters, for without genuine meeting our 'care' becomes the manipulation of other people, treating them as though they were inanimate objects not living persons. But since being present to another is *not* a technique (this would merely be a more subtle form of manipulation), it cannot really be taught. The best that training can achieve is to remove some of the obstacles to such encounters. These obstacles are found in our listening, in our looking, and in our interpreting.

1. At the simplest level we need to learn genuinely to listen to others. This is surprisingly difficult, because of our natural tendency to try to formulate an interpretation of what we hear as quickly as possible to prepare for rapid action. (Hearing, like vision, has a basic survival function, warning of threats in our immediate environment.) Non-egoistic listening is responsiveness to the richness of sound and of meaning which comes from the other. The music of the human voice provides a complex emotional accompaniment to the sense of the words which are uttered. The words and phrases are themselves rich in association of all kinds for the person who uses them. To *hear* another person is to allow ourselves to enter his personal world, where words and the uttering of words have a nuance peculiar to that individual. We can do this only if we learn to free ourselves from distractions to our attention. Paradoxically, this freedom comes not from learning how to concentrate, but from learning how to relax. The untrained helper has as his chief distraction an overwhelming desire to be helpful. As a result he can scarcely hear the other person for the clamour of his own inner voices, which frantically search for a solution, mentally formulating answers to questions which have not even been asked! We are able to listen properly when we can shut off both inner and outer noise and allow the voice of the other person to fill our attention. (The analogy of listening to music with appreciation rather than with half an ear to other sounds may prove helpful.)

2. In a similar way, we pay attention to others by *looking* at them. Such looking is not the same as inquisitive staring, nor as a detached, 'clinical' observation. It is the subtle rhythm of looking and looking away which amplifies and eases our verbal communication.[13] To be present to another person is to offer them the openness of our face, to catch, but not to imprison, their eyes, and to allow ourselves to see them

103

in all the vitality of their bodily expressiveness. Training can improve our awareness of the nuances of 'body language', but the purpose of such increased sensitization must always be to make us better participants in truly personal communication. As soon as we use such training as a source of 'cleverness', placing us in the position of the sophisticated observer of behaviour, we insulate ourselves from I-Thou encounter. The looking which enhances such encounter comes from the desire to know, not to know *about*, the other person.

3. Another major obstacle to knowledge of others comes from our need to make sense of the world by discerning regularities. As Hume convincingly demonstrated, the basis of all science is the prediction of the future through observation of regularities in the past. The whole notion of 'sciences of man' depends upon the extension of this principle to human behaviour. Thus psychology searches for the laws which regulate the motivation, cognition and behaviour of the individual, whilst sociology seeks out similar regularities operating at the level of social groups and whole societies. The basic assumption of all studies of this kind is that we can understand particular events more adequately by seeing their place within a general pattern of predictable regularity. This mode of understanding is undeniably useful. It alerts us to features of human interaction which, without such theoretical grounding, we might easily overlook,[14] and it enables us to make plans for appropriate facilities to meet broad areas of human need.[15] But the extension of the 'scientific' approach to individual caring relationships has grave dangers. As soon as we regard the person before us as one example of a whole set of similar 'cases' we blind ourselves to the uniqueness of his need for care. We restrict ourselves to offering a functional relationship, in which our task becomes the matching of the correct treatment to the problem before us.

Of course, there *are* such regularities in human need. People respond to illness, bereavement, 'life crises' of various kinds in broadly similar ways. An awareness of these regularities (such as the 'grief process' in bereavement)[16] may help us to avoid inappropriate reactions to behaviour which we cannot immediately understand. But the primary mode of our relating must be one which shuns generalizations about people's 'problems'. Since pastoral care has to do with mutuality, not with professional 'know how', with sharing not with solving, it is more important to respond to the uniqueness of the other person than to classify his similarities with others. This means resisting our desire for order and coherence, and allowing the strangeness and newness of *this* person's experience to clutter up our attention. We naturally dislike this kind of 'untidiness', because it threatens our control of the situation. In abandoning classifications we abandon ourselves to the moment, uncertain how we can cope with the immediacy of this person's unhappiness, perplexity or fear. Yet it is precisely such moments of immediate presence which restore the wholeness we both lack. Some more words by Buber capture this essential point:

> Only the view of what is over against me in the world in its full presence, with which I have set myself in relation, present in my whole person – only this view gives me the world truly and wholly as one.[17]

It follows that preparation for pastoral care must go beyond the definition of 'problems' to an attempt to come to grips with that fundamental lack in our lives, our inability to share experience with others at anything other than the most superficial level. Such sharing requires a *context* and a *medium of communication*. The context is community, in its fundamental sense of a small number of individuals bound together by a common concern. The medium (as I have been suggesting throughout this book) is the active imagination, which responds with delight to the unfamiliar, the unexpected, the cross-grained, the unclassifiable.

A path to the rediscovery of pastoral care in church life and in theological education will be found only when there is a willingness to risk new ways of learning about others and new ways of sharing with others. Often we prefer to hold on to the old wine for fear of cracking those dried-up, but comfortingly familiar wineskins which we inherited from past generations. The new wine requires changes in our church structures, our educational methods and our ways of relating. These changes must include the abandoning of the pointless formality of institutions which are forever taking themselves too seriously, the integration in church life of the tranquillity of old age with the freshness and spontaneity of youth, the rediscovery of the *bodily* nature of sacramental grace, and (above all) the re-creation of a worship whose relaxation and repose give space and time for loving God and others.

SOLITUDE

A final path to the rediscovery of pastoral care goes in a surprising direction – to a place of solitude. We must not suppose that all our resources for caring will come from relationships with others. Important as such supportive and challenging experiences are, we must also learn to be alone and not to fear such solitude. Solitude must be distinguished from loneliness. The pain of loneliness comes when we feel shut off from other people, longing for their company but somehow unable to gain it. The lonely person feels totally powerless, a victim of circumstance. It may be his own timidity which prevents him from finding the warmth of companionship, but he cannot see a way of crossing the gulf between himself and others. Such loneliness often comes in old age or after bereavement, when the close relationships upon which the person depended have been removed and no new ones have taken their place. The lonely person needs help, though the very private character of his need often means that no one notices his distress. He needs to recover a sense of being loved and cared for and of being a person who has something to give to others. But the person who seeks solitude does so out of a deliberate intention to be alone. He absents himself from the company of others for a while, not because he dislikes or despises such company, but because he knows the great value of solitude. Like Jesus, alone for a night of prayer on the mountain (Luke 6:12), the seeker after solitude needs times away from people, even from those closest to him, in order to enter his inner depths, in which God's presence is also to be found.

It is unfortunate that a kind of mystique has grown up around the ancient practice of solitude. Obviously there are people whose true vocation is a life of contemplative prayer within some form of monastic community. There are others whose insights in the 'arts' of meditation and contemplation have a profound and universal appeal, making them into helpful 'spiritual guides' for others. But solitude is in essence an utterly simple experience, one immediately accessible to everyone. All that it requires is a willingness to step aside from daily activity (perhaps only for a few moments) in order to regain contact with the 'still centre' of our being.[18] Most of our days are spent in fragmented activity, the focusing of a *part* of ourselves to the task at hand, leaving out of view the rich variety of our whole being. Times of solitude allow a 'return to the centre', when all parts of us have an equal right to be, no part clamouring for expression above another, and when that mysterious unity we call 'self' finds its place in the unity of all things grounded in God. The unity is there always: to recognize our singleness, to be alone with God, is to find it.[19]

The person who knows even a little of such solitude will be better prepared to offer care to others. In the previous chapter I discussed the uncertainties in each person's journey of faith and the need for companionship. Paradoxically, solitude aids companionship. The good companion possesses a calmness which comes from within. He knows the seriousness that is different from solemnity and the laughter that comes from simple things. The good companion is not uneasy with silence, because he has known it as a good friend. He may not see the end of life's journey clearly, yet somehow it feels to him like returning home, because home has been all around him in his moments of peace within himself. Yet the person who knows solitude also knows fear and pain, for (as all the literature on mystical experience testifies) times of solitude may also lead to a 'dark night of the soul', when we feel abandoned and vulnerable, surrounded by deep and terrifying darkness. Thus the practice of solitude equips us as battle comrades also, as healers who know their own wounds, as leaders who have often wished to run from danger. All these shades of light and dark are within the unity that lies in those depths of self that is also not-self, those depths from which God's vast creation springs.

Thus preparation for pastoral care must avoid the danger of superficiality, of dealing only with techniques or with the more obvious dimensions of human need. We struggle to plumb the depths of human experience in pastoral care. Formation for pastoral care must therefore encourage people to pay attention to the 'inner life', in times of quiet reflection which give leave for light or dark to enter in. This is not the 'spiritual solace' of the person who wants to nurse his wounds in private, hiding from life's cruelties, nor the self-righteousness of the person seeking to prove his piety to God and to fellow men. The path of solitude leads to the rediscovery of pastoral care, because it fills our hearts with the rich simplicity of God:

Look to your heart
that flutters in and out like a moth
God is not indifferent to your need.
You have a thousand prayers
but God has one.[20]

Notes And References

Scripture References:
All Scripture references are included in the main text. The following
abbreviations are used to indicate versions.
AV .... Authorized Version
JB .... Jerusalem Bible
NEB .... New English Bible
TEV .... Today's English Version (Good News Bible).

Chapter One
1. See an early criticism of this trend in T. C. Oden's assessment
   of the American literature on pastoral care in *Contemporary Theology and Psychotherapy* (Westminster Press 1967), pp. 57f.
2. Cox, H., *Turning East* (Simon & Schuster, New York, 1978),
   p. 159.
3. Oden, Thomas C., 'Freedom to Learn', a paper presented to
   the International Congress on Pastoral Care and Counselling,
   Edinburgh 1979. Reprinted in W. Becher, G. K. Parker, and
   A. V. Campbell, ed., *The Risks of Freedom* (in press). See also
   Oden's paper, 'Recovering Lost Identity', *Journal of Pastoral
   Care*, vol. xxiv, No. 1 (March 1980), in which he argues for a
   re-integration of the insights of the 'classical tradition', an en-
   riched synthesis of old and new in pastoral care. Some of the
   oversimplifications in Oden's view are well observed by E. V.
   Stein in his commentary on the paper, but the general aims
   Oden espouses seem admirable. It remains to be seen how
   specifically he will implement them in future writings.
4. Clebsch, William A. and Jaekle, Charles R., *Pastoral Care in
   Historical Perspective* (Harper Torchbooks 1967), Preface to the
   Torchbook Edition and pp. 73ff.
5. 'The Incarnate One', *Collected Poems. 1921–1958* (Faber and Faber 1960), p. 228.
6. Baxter, R., *Gildas Silvianus or The Reformed Pastor* (First pub.
   1655; Nisbet 1860). Baxter was an English Puritan, but his
   work had a widespread influence in the Reformed churches.

7. Thurneysen, Eduard, *A Theology of Pastoral Care* (John Knox Press 1962), p. 15.

8. Fairbairn, Patrick, *Pastoral Theology* (T. & T. Clark 1875), p. 297.

9. See Tillich, Paul, *The Dynamics of Faith* (Harper & Row, New York, 1957), for one of the clearest expositions of this viewpoint in relation to Christian belief. The writings of Liam Hudson (see for example *Frames of Mind* (Methuen 1968)) present the case for tolerance of ambiguity from the perspective of educational psychology.

10. Thus T. F. Torrance explains the importance of catechisms as follows: 'Christianity is above all the question the Truth puts to man at every point in his life, so that it teaches him to ask the right, the true questions about himself. . . . Now the Catechism is designed to do just this, and it is therefore an invaluable method in instructing the young learner, for it not only trains him to ask the right questions, but trains him to allow himself to be questioned by the Truth . . .' (*The School of Faith*, James Clarke 1959, p. xxvi). We note here a conviction that theological orthodoxy, as the author defines it, is to be equated with a true knowledge of God, whilst the spiritual quest of individuals, unaided by that orthodoxy, is seen as incapable even of asking the right questions.

11. See for example Oates, Wayne, *Protestant Pastoral Counselling* (Westminster Press 1962). But Jay Adams (*Competent to Counsel* (Presbyterian Reformed Publishing Company 1977)) tries to make old style directiveness sound like professional counselling by coining a neologism: 'nouthetic' counselling.

12. Clebsch and Jaekle, op. cit., pp. 316–18.

13. For an introduction to and selections from Knox's Liturgy see Clebsch and Jaekle, ibid., pp. 253–61.

14. G. D. Henderson paints a lively picture of the practice in its heyday: 'At Cullen on a certain Sunday in 1664 there were on the stool a woman (in sackcloth) making her fifth appearance, a woman (seventh), a man (fifth), a man and two women (fourth), two women (third), and a man making his first appearance, nine persons in all.'
Not everyone, however, treated the occasion with the expected penitent attitude: 'Some delinquents took the matter lightly or appeared to do so, and we have stories of the wearing of disguises, of the breaking of the stool, of impertinent remarks and of an air of bravado.' *The Scottish Ruling Elder* (James Clarke 1935), pp. 116ff.

15. Fairbairn, op. cit., p. 344.

16. Clebsch and Jaekle, op. cit., p. 257.

17. Ibid., p. 306.
18. Berdyaev, Nicolas, *Spirit and Reality* (Geoffrey Bles: The Century Press 1939), p. 98.
19. Hillman, James, *Insearch: Psychology and Religion* (Hodder & Stoughton 1967), p. 13.
20. Perhaps the most influential statement of this is in C. R. Rogers' essays on the topic, 'How can I be of help?', published in *On Becoming a Person* (Houghton-Mifflin 1961), in which 'empathy', 'acceptance', and 'congruence' are identified as essential qualities in the counsellor. These ideas are more fully explored in Chapter Six below.
21. Rogers, C. R., ibid., pp. 32f.
22. See especially his *Pastoral Counselling* (Abingdon, New York, 1949).
23. Kazantzakis, Nikos, *The Last Temptation* (Faber and Faber 1979, paperback edition), pp. 161f.
24. Shaw, Bernard, *Saint Joan* (Penguin Books 1946), p. 165.
25. See especially *The Integration of the Personality* (Kegan Paul 1940), and *Modern Man in Search of a Soul* (Routledge and Kegan Paul 1961).
26. 'The Stages of Life' in *Modern Man in Search of a Soul*, pp. 119f.
27. Yeats W. B., 'The Second Coming', *The Collected Poems of W. B. Yeats* (Macmillan 1960), p. 184.
28. Merton, Thomas, *Contemplative Prayer* (Darton, Longman & Todd 1973), p. 38.
29. A notable attempt to describe the uniqueness of pastoral counselling has been made by H. J. Clinebell, *Basic Types of Pastoral Counselling* (Chapter Three), but his argument is based on the assumption that a trained ministry will provide pastoral counselling. In my discussion of pastoral care I am deliberately departing from the idea that it is (in any special sense) the function of the ministry alone to offer care.

Chapter Two
1. *Four Quartets* (Faber paperback edition 1959), p. 19.
2. Hudson, Liam, *Frames of Mind* (Methuen 1968).
3. See Ornstein, Robert, *The Psychology of Consciousness* (W. H. Freeman, San Francisco, 1972). But such building of theory upon slender evidence about 'two hemisphere' thinking is open to criticism. See for example Popper, K. R., Eccles, J. C., *The Self and its Brain* (Springer International, Berlin, 1977).
4. Plato, *The Republic*, Books 2 and 10.
5. Although I have not referred to it directly, the account of image, symbol and myth in James Mackey's *Jesus, the Man and the Myth*

(SCM 1979) has been influential in my description of the transcendent character of some images.

6. Tillich, Paul, *The Dynamics of Faith* (Harper Row, New York, 1957).
7. *Systematic Theology*, vol. 1 (Chicago U.P. 1973), p. 265.
8. Buber, Martin, *Images of Good and Evil* (Routledge & Kegan Paul 1952), p. 37.
9. Ibid., p. 42.
10. Lynch, William F., *Christ and Apollo: The Dimensions of the Literary Imagination* (Sheed & Ward 1960), p. 7.
11. Ibid., p. 19, author's italics.
12. Such goals are implicit or explicit in the writings of Seward Hiltner, Carroll Wise, Paul E. Johnson and Howard J. Clinebell.
13. From different theological perspectives Eduard Thurneysen and Jay E. Adams both deny any capacity to human imagination or insight. (For references see footnotes 7 and 11 in Chapter One above.)
14. I am indebted to my wife Sally for this example. See Campbell, Sally B., 'Fragmentation and Wholeness', Certificate in Pastoral Studies Dissertation, unpublished, University of Edinburgh 1980.
15. For example, in the Old Testament God's loving care is expressed through the covenant relationship, but I have not explored this imagery. Similarly *servanthood* and *sonship* are central biblical motifs, which deserve closer attention in discussing pastoral care. See Brister, C. W., *Pastoral Care in the Church* (Harper & Row 1964), Chapter One.

Chapter Three

1. Darton, Longman & Todd 1973, p. 25.
2. Kittel, G., *Theological Dictionary of the New Testament* (Eerdmans 1968), vol. vi, p. 487.
3. E.g. Ps. 23:1–4; Jer. 23:3; Ezek. 34: 11–22; Isa. 40: 10f. See also Micah 4: 6–8.
4. There is a very early tradition about the birth place being a cave (see Kittel, op. cit., p. 491), a common animal shelter in those times. On the other hand, Luke's preference for supernatural revelations probably means that (as 2:15 seems to imply) we are to suppose that it was from the angels that the shepherds learned the location of the manger.
5. The Greek verb used (*proagein*) is ambiguous in meaning. It could mean simply 'go ahead of you', in the sense of 'go there earlier in time than you'. If so, the shepherding reference is less definite.

6. Reference is sometimes made to the investing of Peter with a 'pastoral office' (John 21: 15–19). However, such an interpretation does not equate well with the stress elsewhere in John on the priority of the relationship between the *individual* believer and Jesus. In any case this passage appears to be a later addition to the Gospel. See Dunn, J. G., *Unity and Diversity in the New Testament* (SCM 1977), pp. 118f, and p. 398, n. 20.

7. See Vinet, A., *Pastoral Theology* (T. & T. Clark 1852); and Fairbairn, P., *Pastoral Theology* (T. & T. Clark 1875), for examples of this approach.

8. E.g. J. J. van Oosterzee, *Practical Theology* (Hodder & Stoughton 1878).

9. See for example the emphasis on professionalism in his discussion of 'The Layman as Pastoral Theologian' in *Preface to Pastoral Theology* (Abingdon, New York, 1958), pp. 37–9.

10. An expansion of this criticism will be found in my article, 'Is Practical Theology Possible?', *Scottish Journal of Theology* 25, 2 (May 1972).

11. See Chapter Two of *The Christian Shepherd* (Abingdon, New York, 1959); and also Chapter One of *Preface to Pastoral Theology*.

12. These parables are referred to briefly in *The Christian Shepherd*.

13. The phrase 'inner strength' might be regarded as a psychologizing of the Gospel narrative. Apart from occasional references in Luke we get few clues from the evangelists about Jesus' inner state. But the point I have in mind is the decisiveness of Jesus' declarations of God's love, which spring (in the Johannine account) from his assertion: 'I and the Father are one.' This conviction seems to demonstrate the 'integrity' I have already described in Chapter One above and allows me to speak of the steadfastness of Jesus' character.

14. See Oates, W. E., *When Religion Gets Sick* (Westminster 1970).

Chapter Four

1. *The Peacock and the Phoenix* (Celestial Arts, Millbrae California, 1975).

2. This point has been well made by Martin Buber in dialogue with Carl Rogers. Buber insists that professional psychotherapy cannot be the same as an I-Thou encounter, because of the inequality entailed. See *The Knowledge of Man* (Allen & Unwin 1965), Appendix.

3. This is not to deny the usefulness of both knowledge and skill in certain situations, but training in pastoral care – so far as it is necessary – must be mostly concerned with *attitudes* (to oneself and to others). See Chapter Eight below.

4. Shillito, E., 'Jesus of the Scars' in Morrison, J. D., ed. *Master-pieces of Religious Verse* (Harper & Row, New York, 1948).
5. *The Crucified God* (SCM 1974), p. 252.
6. *Revelations of Divine Love* (Penguin Classics 1966), p. 71.
7. *Insearch* (Hodder & Stoughton 1967), p. 18.
8. *The Merchant of Venice*, Act III, Scene I. The question is poign-ant, for it reflects both a protest against anti-Semitism and a determination to be as vengeful as his persecutors: 'and if you wrong us, shall we not revenge?'
9. Maimonides, *Prayer of a Physician*.
10. Shannon, op. cit., (see note 1 above), p. 116.
11. For a discussion of death as *both* friend and enemy see my essay, 'The Meaning of Death and Ministry to the Dying' in Doyle, D., ed., *Terminal Care* (Churchill Livingstone 1979).
12. *Insearch*, loc. cit.
13. *Devotions upon Emergent Occasions*, No. xvii (1623).
14. Few writers have described these experiences more effectively than Erik H. Erikson. See especially *Childhood and Society* (Penguin Books 1965). A discussion of Erikson's developmental the-ory and of its relationship to 'the journey of faith' will be found in Chapter Seven below.
15. For a full and sensitive treatment of this topic (and for many practical guidelines for pastoral care) see Fairchild, R. W., *Finding Hope Again* (Harper & Row, New York, 1980).
16. *The Wounded Healer* (Doubleday & Co., New York, 1972), p. 94.
17. Thus Freud could make a convincing case for religion as a defensive system. See *The Future of an Illusion* (Hogarth Press 1970, first published 1927).
18. *The Christian Shepherd* (Abingdon, New York, 1959), p. 44.
19. Cryer, N. S. and Vayhinger, J. M., *Casebook in Pastoral Counseling* (Abingdon, New York, 1962), pp. 63–5.
20. 'Now the green blade riseth from the buried grain.' Hymn by John Macleod Campbell Crum, *The Church Hymnary*, 3rd edn (Oxford University Press 1973), No. 278.
21. Alexander Solzhenitsyn's novel, *One Day in the Life of Ivan Den-isovich*, conveys in a mysterious way a sense of hope and tran-scendence in the conditions of a Siberian work camp, where no hope seems possible. It is a moving portrayal of a community of sufferers who have only the harshest of realities to experience. Yet the principal character can say at the end of his day: 'A day without a dark cloud. Almost a happy day.'
22. Eliot, T. S., 'East Coker', *Four Quartets* (Faber Paperback Edi-tion 1959) p. 29f.

Chapter Five

1. *The Faber Book of Modern Verse*, ed. Michael Roberts (Faber and Faber 1960), p. 61.
2. See Welsford, E., *The Fool: His Society and Literary History* (Faber and Faber 1935); and Willeford, W., *The Fool and His Sceptre* (Edward Arnold 1969); Saward J., *Perfect Fools* (OUP 1980).
3. *The Journals of Kierkegaard 1834–1854*, ed. and tr. Alexander Dru (Collins Fontana 1958), p. 54.
4. *Philosophical Fragments*, tr. David F. Swenson (Princeton University Press 1936), p. 50.
5. *The Exploits of the Incomparable Mulla Nasrudin* (Pan Picador edn 1973), p. 22.
6. *As You Like It*, Act V, Scene 4.
7. *Praise of Folly*, or *Moriae Encomium*. The original Latin title enshrines a pun, since the work was dedicated to his friend Thomas More.
8. *Praise of Folly*, tr. Betty Radice (Penguin Classics 1971), p. 201. The work was written while Erasmus was a guest in More's home and was first published two years later, in 1511.
9. Ibid., p. 198.
10. See Welsford, op. cit., Part II.
11. Dostoyevsky, F., *The Idiot*, tr. David Magarshack (Penguin 1955), p. 149.
12. Peter Sellers' last film, 'Being There', is a brilliant portrayal of how simplicity can lay bare society's folly. The principal character, Chance, played by Sellers himself, becomes regarded as a financial wizard, fit to be presidential adviser and even presidential candidate. Yet throughout the film, Chance, the gardener (elevated into 'Chauncey Gardner') is speaking at his own simple level about gardening and about the way he feels about people. His 'brilliance' is the fabrication of the folly of those around him.
13. *King Lear*, Act III, Scene 1.
14. Ibid., Act II, Scene 4.
15. The heroism of the fool is always tempered by his fearfulness and his dislike of the uncomfortable state which 'nuncle' has got them both into. He remains convincingly a Court Fool, but one whose loyalty evokes high praise from some commentators: e.g. 'He is the supremely wise fool who expresses in his heartfelt devotion to Cordelia and to his King the Christian virtues of patience, humility and love' (Goldsmith, R. H., *Wise Fools in Shakespeare* (Liverpool University Press 1958), p. 67). See also Kaiser, W., *Praisers of Folly* (Victor Gollancz 1964), p. 99.
16. For a discussion of the pathos in clowning see Disher, M.W., *Clowns and Pantomines* (Constable 1925), especially his study of

Grock (pp. 203 ff). The clown paintings of Georges Rouault are also illuminating in this regard.

17. See Lindblom, J., *Prophecy in Ancient Israel* (Blackwell 1962), pp. 1f.

18. Zucker, W. M. 'The Clown as the Lord of Disorder', *Theology To-day*, vol. xxiv, No. 3 (October 1967), p. 316.

19. See Cox, H., *The Feast of Fools* (Harvard University Press 1969), p. 3; Welsford op. cit., pp. 199 ff; Zucker, op. cit., p. 313.

20. For a complete list see Fohrer, G., *History of Israelite Religion*, tr. D. E. Green (SPCK 1973), p. 240. Fohrer suggests that such actions had their antecedents in magic, but that the prophets used them not in connection with sorcery but as proclamations of God's power and divine intention. A similar viewpoint is expressed by Lindblom, op. cit., p. 172.

21. Commentators save Isaiah's modesty by suggesting that his mantle would not be discarded (Lindblom, ibid., p. 169, n. 101).

22. There has been some dispute about whether the accounts in Hosea are intended to be historical narrative, but most modern critics believe them to be. See Lindblom, ibid., pp. 165–9.

23. Stiven, Tessa, 'The Fool' in *Poetry of Persons* (Limited edn publ. by the Quarto Press, 69 Swan Road, Feltham, Middlesex, 1976).

24. It is significant that these teachings and actions are all reported in Luke's Gospel, since Luke was particularly concerned to show that Jesus was more than simply the fulfilment of *Jewish* messianic expectations. See Caird, G.B., *Saint Luke* (Penguin 1963), Introduction.

25. For a discussion of the humour in Jesus' teaching, see Trueblood, E., *The Humour of Christ* (Harper, New York, 1964).

26. The mischievous figure of Harlequin is a good example of this type of folly. His main qualities were 'agility, resilience and, as a rule, complete absence of moral sense' (Welsford, op. cit., p. 299). In this context, it is odd to find Harvey Cox, in an otherwise imaginative and well-researched study, using Harlequin as a title for Christ! (Cox, H., op. cit.).

27. See Disher, M. W., op. cit., p. xiii: 'Satisfy people's desire for the ridiculous and they will accept your idea of the sublime.' In *Homo Ludens* (Routledge & Kegan Paul 1949), J. Huizinga points out that while human beings are not unique in their delight in play, their capacity for laughter sets them apart from the other animals.

28. *Pastoral Care in the Modern Hospital* (SCM Press 1971), pp. 81–92.

29. Miller, S. H., 'The Clown in Contemporary Art', *Theology Today*, XXIV, 3 (Oct. 1967) p. 327.
30. The danger of professionalism in caring is fully discussed in Illich, I., *Disabling Professions* (Boyars 1978). A thorough critique of the moves towards standardization and accreditation in pastoral care will be found in Lambourne, R. A., 'Objections to a National Pastoral Organisation', *Contact* 35 (June 1971).
31. Gibran, K., *The Prophet*. (Heinemann 1976), p. 71.
32. Blake, William, 'Auguries of Innocence', in *A Choice of Blake's Verse* selected by Kathleen Raine (Faber & Faber 1970).
33. Eliot, T. S., *Four Quartets* (Faber & Faber 1959), p. 59.
34. *King Lear*, Act I, Scene 4.
35. See Nouwen, H. J., *The Living Reminder* (Seabury, New York, 1977), for a most helpful discussion of the pastoral significance of the absence of Jesus.
36. Watts, A., *Beyond Theology: The Art of Godmanship* (Vintage Books, New York, 1973), p. 211.
37. 'If the Lord is said to veil his glory, lest it be too bright for mortal eyes, might he not also veil his mirth – perhaps as something much, much too funny for men to stand?' (ibid., p. 54).
38. Stiven, T., loc. cit.

Chapter Six

1. *The Marriage of Heaven and Hell*, etched about 1793. Selections published in Pinto, Vo. de Sola, ed., *William Blake* (Batsford 1965), p. 102.
2. See Menninger, K., *Whatever Became of Sin?* (Hodder & Stoughton 1973).
3. Mowrer, O.H., *The Crisis in Psychiatry and Religion* (Van Norstrand 1961), p. 121. A more cautious description of the disappearance of the concepts of sin and guilt in modern society can be found in Menninger, K., *Whatever Became of Sin?*, but Menninger, like Mowrer, makes a too simple equation of changing views of morality and loss of morality.
4. My discussion of this vast topic is inevitably brief and oversimplified. For a full and scholarly discussion of the issues see Stein, E.V., *Guilt: Theory and Therapy* (Westminster 1968). Other useful works are France, M., *The Paradox of Guilt* (Hodder & Stoughton 1967); and McKenzie, J. G., *Guilt: its Meaning and Significance* (Abingdon, New York, 1962).
5. Freud, S., *New Introductory Lectures on Psychoanalysis* (Penguin 1973), p. 112.
6. Of course, other psychiatric theorists would ascribe depression

to biochemical factors rather than intrapsychic ones, but, whichever theory is correct, the irrelevance of the severe feelings of guilt to morality equally applies.

7. Rogers, C. R., *On Becoming a Person* (Houghton Mifflin 1961), Chapter 8. The phrase is borrowed from Kierkegaard's *The Concept of Dread*, but with no awareness apparently of how ironically Kierkegaard is using it.

8. Rogers, ibid., p. 34.

9. Ibid., Chapters 8 and 9.

10. Ibid., p. 194.

11. See Oden, T. C., *Kerygma and Counselling* (Westminster Press 1966), Chapter 3: 'The Theology of Carl Rogers'.

12. Certainly Rogers speaks of 'I-Thou' encounter when trying to explain why the therapeutic relationship is effective, but he uses this purely as a means to the autonomy of the individual. Although he uses the terminology of Martin Buber, his view of man lacks Buber's category of the inter-human and he ignores entirely the element of *confrontation by the other*, so essential to Buber's anthropology.

13. Berdyaev, N., *Spirit and Reality* (Geoffrey Bles 1946), p. 69.

14. *Gitanjali* (Macmillan India 1973, 1st edn 1913), No. xcii, p. 61.

15. See Cole, W. G., *Sex in Christianity and Psychoanalysis* (Oxford 1955); Watts, A., *Nature, Man and Woman* (Sphere Books 1976); Nelson, J. B., *Embodiment: An Approach to Sexuality and Christian Theology* (SPCK 1979).

16. Luther, M., 'A Sermon on the Estate of Marriage', *Collected Works*, vol. 44, pp. 1–14.

17. Watts, A., op. cit., (note 15 above), p. 145.

18. See *Journal of Medical Ethics* (1980), 6, 2. Similarly women undergoing hysterectomies or mastectomies experience an overwhelming sense of mutilation.

19. The use of the masculine possessive pronoun here is misleading and unfortunate. I use it only because of a dislike of the clumsiness of 'his/her', etc. Throughout the discussion I am intending to refer equally to men and women, despite the grammar.

20. See Austin, C. R., 'Bisexuality and the problem of its social acceptance', *Journal of Medical Ethics* (1978), 4, 132–7.

21. Jung, C. G., 'The Relations between the Ego and the Unconscious', *Two Essays on Analytical Psychology* (Meridian Books 1956), p. 199.

22. Nelson, J. B., op. cit. (See note 15 above), p. 102.

23. The late Fritz Perls has drawn attention to this in his writing on Gestalt Therapy. See Fagan, J., and Shepherd, I. L., *Gestalt Therapy Now* (Palo Alto California, Science and Behaviour Books, 1970).

Chapter Seven
1. *Four Quartets* (Faber & Faber 1959), p. 13.
2. Hesse, H., *Siddhartha* (Pan Books, Picador edn, 1973).
3. Ibid., p. 108.
4. See Dalrymple, J., *Longest Journey* (Darton, Longman & Todd 1979).
5. *Philosophical Fragments*, tr. D. F. Swenson (Princeton University Press 1936), p. 5.
6. Ibid., p. 25.
7. Ibid., Chapter 4, 'The Case of the Contemporary Disciple'.
8. Thus Kierkegaard believes that we need almost nothing in the way of testimony from the contemporaries of Jesus: 'If the contemporary generation had left nothing behind them but these words: "We have believed that in such and such a year God appeared among us in the humble figure of a servant, that he lived and taught in our community, and finally died", it would be more than enough' (ibid., p. 87).
9. See *The Dynamics of Faith* (Harper Row, New York, 1957).
10. Maslow, A., *Towards a Psychology of Being* (Van Norstrand 1962), Preface.
11. A good summary of these self-actualization theories is given in 'The Personal Imperative' by John W. Shaw in Ruddock, R., ed., *Six Approaches to the Person* (Routledge & Kegan Paul 1972).
12. *Motivation and Personality* (Harper & Bros. 1954); *Towards a Psychology of Being* (Van Norstrand 1962); *Religious Values and Peak Experiences* (Viking Press 1964); *The Farther Reaches of Human Nature* (Penguin Books 1973).
13. *The Farther Reaches of Human Nature*, p. 50.
14. Ibid., p. 45.
15. Cf. Viktor Frankl's concept of 'existential frustration'. *See Man's Search for Meaning* (Washington Square Press, New York, 1963); and *Psychotherapy and Existentialism* (Penguin 1973).
16. See *Childhood and Society* (Penguin Books 1965), Chapter Seven; and *Identity, Youth and Crisis* (Faber and Faber 1968), Chapter Three.
17. See *Insight and Responsibility* (Faber and Faber 1964).
18. Erikson's account of these later stages in life is clearly influenced by C. G. Jung's observation that 'Among all my patients in the second half of life – that is to say, over thirty-five – there has not been one whose problem in the last resort was not that of finding a religious outlook on life' (*Modern Man in Search of a Soul* (Routledge & Kegan Paul 1961), p. 264).
19. *Childhood and Society*, p. 261.
20. This aspect of pastoral caring is well developed in Henri Nouwen, *The Living Reminder* (Seabury Press, New York, 1977).

21. Tillich, Paul, 'You Are Accepted', in *The Shaking of the Foundations* (SCM 1949).
22. Tagore Rabindranath, *Gitanjali* (Macmillan India 1974), p. 29.
23. In an amusing and perceptive essay, 'The Enjoyment of Living', a modern Chinese writer, Lin Yutang, writes in praise of lying in bed as a source of both physical and spiritual refreshment. Since the body is completely relaxed, the mind is open to new ideas, and the senses (especially hearing and smell) are more acute. Lin Yutang particularly recommends waking at dawn to listen to the bird songs, hardly the advice of a lazy man! (See *The Importance of Living* (Heinemann 1938), Chapter 9.)
24. *Macbeth*, Act V, Scene 5.
25. St Francis of Assisi, 'All creatures of our God and King', *The Church Hymnary*, 3rd edn (OUP 1973), No. 30.
26. Kazantzakis, N., *Report to Greco* (Simon & Schuster, New York, 1965).
27. E. Kübler-Ross has described anger as a necessary stage in coming to 'acceptance' of death. See *On Death and Dying* (Tavistock 1973). While not disagreeing with this, the fight I have in mind has more to do with questions of transcendence than her psychological analysis can suggest.
28. Eliot, T. S., 'Little Gidding', op. cit,. p. 59.

Chapter Eight

1. Darton, Longman & Todd 1973, p. 26. Merton is referring to the monastic vocation, but he also makes it clear that his words apply to all Christian vocation.
2. The inverted commas are well-advised! I am aware that these are vague terms and that there is much debate about the possible status of theology as a 'science'.
3. See Bloom, B. S., ed., *Taxonomy of Educational Objectives* (Longmans 1956).
4. *Images of Faith* (University of Notre Dame Press 1973), p. 20.
5. For a useful description of the pitfalls created by the unacknowledged needs of the 'helping personality', see Eadie, H. A., 'The Helping Personality', *Contact* 49 (Summer 1975).
6. Ken Kesey's novel (and the subsequent film), *One Flew Over The Cuckoo's Nest* (Pan Picador 1973), is a brilliant portrayal of the danger.
7. In using the term 'confession' I wish to stress the religious significance of such searching of motives. Sometimes the use of supervised training of this type is regarded as an intrusion of psychotherapeutic methods into theological education. But as Carl Jung observed (see 'Psychotherapists or the Clergy?', *Mod-*

ern Man in Search of a Soul (Routledge & Kegan Paul 1961)), psychotherapy is merely a secularization of the ancient insights of the confessional. The point is to make such modern 'confessionals' a way to gracefulness rather than an encouragement to self-denigration (see Chapter Six above).

8. Modern methods of pastoral supervision are well summarized and evaluated in Klink, T. W., 'Supervision', Chapter Six of Feilding, C. R., *Education for Ministry* (American Association of Theological Schools, Dayton Ohio, 1966).

9. Op. cit., p. 129.

10. Quoist, M., *Prayers of Life* (Gill & Son, Dublin, 1963), p. 91.

11. *Between Man and Man* (Collins Fount Paperback 1979), p. 72.

12. The problem of perception is extensively discussed in modern psychology. Brief summaries of the interpretive and selective nature of perception will be found in Ornstein, R. E., *The Psychology of Consciousness* (W. H. Freeman, San Francisco, 1972); and in Medcof, J. and Roth, J., ed., *Approaches to Psychology* (Open University Press 1979), Chapter One.

13. See Argyle, M., *The Psychology of Interpersonal Behaviour* (Penguin 1967), Chapter Six.

14. For example, the sociology of religion has drawn attention to correlations between church membership and social class and to numerous other social influences on religious practice.

15. An example would be changes in facilities for children separated from their parents. Psychological research has demonstrated the damaging effects of large, impersonal institutions.

16. See Parkes, C. M., *Bereavement* (Penguin 1975); Spiegel J., *The Grief Process* (SCM Press 1978).

17. *The Knowledge of Man* (Allen & Unwin 1965), p. 63.

18. This 'still centre' eludes rational description. See Griffiths, B., *Return to the Centre* (Collins Fontana 1978); Dalrymple, J., *Longest Journey* (Darton, Longman & Todd 1979); and Merton, T., op. cit., for sensitive and simple attempts to point to it.

19. Such simplicity is also, of course, profoundly disturbing, for to discover such grounding in all things is also to find our individuality radically questioned. For a helpful discussion of this dimension of self-relinquishment see N. D. O'Donoghue, 'This Noble Noughting and This High Alling', *Journal of Studies in Mysticism* 2, 1 (Autumn 1972), pp. 1–15.

20. Sexton, Anne, 'Not so. Not so.', in *The Awful Rowing Toward God* (Houghton Mifflin, Boston, 1974).

Index of Names